House Beautiful | STYLE 101

LISA CREGAN

House Beautiful | STYLE 101

400 DESIGNER SECRETS TO A BEAUTIFUL HOME

LISA CREGAN

HEARST BOOKS
New York

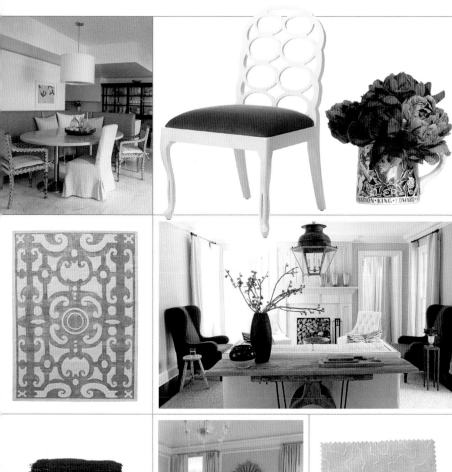

CONTENTS

INTRODUCTION

. . . .

IT'S A COLE PORTER WORLD IN INTERIOR DESIGN
today, literally "Anything Goes." And at *House
Beautiful* we couldn't be more delighted. In our
over hundred-year history, we'd be hard pressed to
name a time when there's been as much innova-
tion, energy, and flat-out rule breaking as there is
in interior design right now.

The upside? Lots of looks to choose from. The
downside? Rank confusion. We thought we might
try sorting things out a bit.

This book aspires to help you define your style,
the first step toward making any kind of décor
decision. Are you a Glam? A New Ruralist? An
Accessorator? A Traditionalist with a Twist? A
Modernist? Don't know what we're talking about?
You soon will.

We're going to draw out the personal style
lurking deep in the nest-building lobe of your
brain. Once you know thy style self, you can get
advice from the pros who fill the pages of *House
Beautiful* every month with invaluable insights,

insider tips, and photos of America's most strikingly beautiful homes.

After seeing where your taste fits in the wide world of style, don't be afraid to color outside our lines. Flipping through these chapters, you're going to find plenty of beautiful, complementary looks that spill over the boundaries of one "style" to another. Let's just say these are more guidelines than rules.

Special thanks to *House Beautiful* editor-in-chief Newell Turner, as well as to all the magazine's talented editors who, month after month, face the impossible task of deciding which gorgeous homes, surprising new products and dazzling designer insights are extraordinary enough for the readers of *House Beautiful*. All you have to do is turn the pages.

Now find your style and get going. It's pretty exciting out there.

— LISA CREGAN

A POP QUIZ

Discover your style

WHY A QUIZ? Here's why: How you answer these questions will determine the style or styles you gravitate toward. And that will clarify every decorating decision you make. No more staring for days at mounds of swatches, no more self-doubting return trips to the paint store for even *more* chips. And most importantly? No more expensive mistakes.

TRUST US. Take out a clean piece of paper and your number 2 pencil (or your flashy glitter gel pen should your style so dictate). We're asking fifteen questions aimed at revealing which design flock you fly with. Total up your answers and then turn to the relevant chapters so we can help you home in on the things you'll love and edit out the stuff that looks great in the showroom, but frankly? just isn't you.

A CAUTIONARY NOTE: We encourage assigning this quiz to your significant other too, but be prepared for some décor differences of opinion.

1. Which dining chair is sexiest?

a. beech with linen slipcover, Darcy from Rachel Ashwell Shabby Chic

b. antique black finish with black velvet seat, Napoleon from Jayson Home & Garden

c. gesso finish with bronze leg collars, from BeeLine Home by Bunny Williams

d. Lucite with tufted seat, George II from Plexi-Craft

e. 1930s design with a lacquer finish, Frances Elkins Side Chair from Downtown

2. My dream bedroom has . . .

a. an antique door for a headboard

b. a canopy bed draped with fabric

c. a steel four-poster

d. crisp ironed sheets

e. a splashy upholstered headboard

a.   b.   c.   d.

4. My idea of the perfect flower arrangement is . . .

a. a small bunch of roses or peonies in a mug

b. fragrant pink sweet peas in a hand painted tole vase

c. deep blue delphiniums in an antique ginger jar

d. a group of bud vases filled with playful anemones

e. fragrant gardenias in a crystal bowl

e.

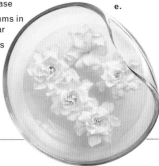

3. If I could only have one window treatment it would be . . .

a. antique shutters

b. silk panels with gold leaf hardware

c. taffeta drapes beneath a shapely fabric valance

d. sheers

e. colorful roman shades

5. My idea of a luxurious tub is . . .

a. a big cast iron tub, Candide Freestanding from WATERWORKS

b. a Chinese white marble number from URBAN ARCHAEOLOGY

c. classical lines by MICHAEL S. SMITH FOR KALLISTA

d. a sleek blue mineral composite tub, ELISE FROM MTI WHIRLPOOLS

e. a sweet yellow clawfoot, MADELINE CLAWFOOT FROM LOWE'S

 a.  b. c. d.

6. I wish my living room had . . .

a. a raw pine-paneled ceiling

b. peacock blue lacquer walls

c. an elegant wainscot

d. a wall of windows

e. lots and lots of built-in bookshelves

7. The movie home I'd most want to live in belonged to . . .

a. Meryl Streep in *Out of Africa*

b. Rosalind Russell in *Auntie Mame*

c. Katherine Hepburn in *The Philadelphia Story*

d. Colin Firth in *A Single Man*

e. Kirsten Dunst in *Marie Antoinette*

8. My dreamhouse is . . .

a. a rose covered cottage by the sea on Nantucket

b. a 1930s Hollywood Regency mansion in Beverly Hills

c. a Georgian townhouse in London

d. a glass-box penthouse over-looking Central Park

e. a 'painted lady' Victorian in San Francisco

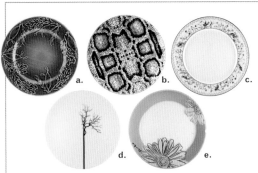

9. Which would you choose?

a. Pinecone from NATURE'S HARVEST

b. Snakeskin from KILN ENAMEL

c. Audubon from TIFFANY & CO.

d. Bodo Sperlein Black Forest from TABLEART

e. Andy Warhol Daisies from ROSENTHAL

10. Which gift would make you happiest (to give or to get)?

a. Platinum and ruby Edwardian pendant

b. Art Deco diamond lion-head earrings

c. Classic white pearl necklace

d. Tiffany gold bangles

e. Vintage Schiaparelli rhinestone ring

11. Pick the item you'd most likely be drawn to in an antique store.

a. a cool industrial cart

b. a statue of a Greek muse

c. a blue-and-white Chinese porcelain vase

d. a Danish mid-century console

e. a green ceramic foo dog

12. Which one of these fabrics makes your heart skip a beat?

a. Woven with jute and finished with a golden sheen. Feuille from SCALAMANDRÉ

b. Satin orchids embroidered on a barely-there background. Orchidea through BERGAMO

c. The iconic quatrefoil, reinvented. Quatrefoil Fern through KOROSEAL

d. A chenille weft and bouclé warp with nuanced texture. Ridgeview from PINDLER & PINDLER

e. A romantic pattern with a modern orange jolt. Brocade from NOMI

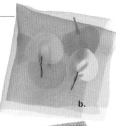
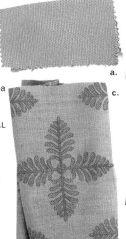

13. **Favorite leading man?**

a. Jeff Bridges

b. Cary Grant

c. Robert Redford

d. Ralph Fiennes

e. Robert Pattinson

14. **Dream vacation spot?**

a. Twin Farms in Barnard, Vermont

b. La Mamounia, Marrakech, Morocco

c. The Ritz, Paris, France

d. The Four Seasons Hotel, New York, New York

e. Pink Sands, Harbour Island, Bahamas

a.

b.

c.

d.

15. **Which throw pillow would jibe with your sofa?**

a. Madeline from Les Indiennes

b. 18th-century Ottoman Empire from B. Viz Design

c. Midnight Ivory Damask from Barclay Butera

d. Bird from k studio

e. Esperanza from Designer's Guild Bed and Bath

e.

WHAT YOUR ANSWERS MEAN

Total up your a, b, c, d and e answers for one point each. Which letter has the most points? That's the one that pinpoints your style. High points for more than one letter? Lucky you—you'll find inspiration everywhere!

MORE "A" answers say you are a **NEW RURALIST** (see page 18)

MORE "B" answers put you in the **GLAM CAMP** (see page 14)

MORE "C" answers tag you a **TRADITIONALIST WITH A TWIST** (see page 22)

MORE "D" answers make you a **MODERNIST** (see page 26)

MORE "E" answers make you an **ACCESSORATOR** (see page 30)

THE GLAM CAMP

You're a style extrovert with confidence that's off the charts. To you, life is theater and your home is the stage. Louis Seize in the mudroom? Roman busts for the front hall? Bring it on! You won't be happy until every single room shimmers with excitement.

YOUR STYLE, DEFINED
Sexy, intense, theatrical.
More is more. There will be
pattern and there will be bling
(and Grecian classics, and
Chinese dynasties, and
perhaps even a little Etruscan).

MUST-HAVES
Mirrors, gilt,
jewel tones, fringe,
crystals, lacquer,
fur, maybe statuary.
Oh, and did we
say gilt?

GO-TO BLOGS
allthebestblog.com
habituallychic.blogspot.com
isuwannee.com
nickolsenstyle.blogspot.com

A FEW GLAM OBSESSIONS

1. **La Solidaridad Stool** by Celestina through Barneys

2. **Milan Buffet** from Shine Home

3. **Mother-of Pearl** Capiz Shell Tiles from Maya Romanoff

4. **Bead Fringe** from Kravet

5. *More is More: Tony Duquette* by Hutton Wilkinson

6. **Jewel Votive** Table Lamp by Tony Duquette through Baker

GLAM
Glossary

TONY DUQUETTE

The indisputable *god of glam fans*. A fearless West Coast–based artist/designer who lined his office with gilded trees and French antiques beneath a glowing ceiling of glued-on gold plastic trays. Glam heaven—all it takes is nerve.

WILLIAM (BILLY) HAINES

Legendary mid-century decorator. He designed a Manhattan penthouse for client Joan Crawford so glam it was called the *"Taj Joan."*

DIANA VREELAND

Late great Vogue editor who famously instructed her decorator to make her New York apartment look like "a *garden* . . . but a garden in Hell."

VICEROY HOTEL, MIAMI

A *glam Mecca*. Is it Modern? Classical? Asian? French? Yes, and 100% glam.

HOLLYWOOD REGENCY

A glam style that worships at the altar of filmdom's most elegant *1930s* movie sets (see Astaire, Fred).

NEW BAROQUE

This gloriously unapologetic reboot of over-the-top *17th-century style*—think curlicues in gilt—offers a fervent *merci beaucoup* to Louis XIV.

"Frankly, I try to force everyone to be more glamorous. I already know what you look like without makeup and that's how I feel about houses. I've seen them without makeup. I know what they look like in the morning. Now let's glam them up!" —MARY McDONALD, DESIGNER

In this dressing room a Regency mirror hangs from the ceiling on chandelier chains.

THE NEW RURALIST

You are a child of nature, drawn to the quiet power of found objects. Silhouette them against ultra-modern surfaces and you love them even more. An antique table, nicked and peeling from the messy reality of living, gets you so much more jazzed than one that's restored and perfect. White-plastered walls and rustic beams blackened by a few centuries' worth of smoke make your heart skip a beat every time you gaze up at them.

YOUR STYLE, DEFINED
Global Country,
pure,
subtly sophisticated,
deep comfort,
boho modern.

MUST-HAVES
Industrial furniture,
antlers,
weathered wood,
focal-point fireplaces, and
miles and miles of linen

GO-TO BLOGS
cotedetexas.blogspot.com
dreamhousecammy.blogspot.com
ruralintelligence.com
southofmarket.biz/blog

A FEW RURALIST OBSESSIONS

1. **Quincy Bed** from Ethan Allen
2. **Cereal Bowl** from Heath Ceramics
3. *THE HOME WITHIN US: The Romantic Houses of McAlpine Tankersley*
4. **Blue Heron Stripe Rug** from Dash & Albert
5. **Wishbone Chair** by Hans Wegner
6. **Haystack Linen Pillow Cover** from Vagabond Vintage

THE NEW RURALIST
Glossary

AXEL VERVOORDT

Belgian *antiques dealer* who's filled his castle with beautifully repurposed ephemera.

SHAKER DICTUM

"Don't make something unless it is *both necessary and useful*; but if it is both necessary and useful, don't hesitate to make it beautiful."

LOCAVORE

Die-hard new ruralists believe there's no soil like *local soil*. If it's not at the farmers' market, they'll plant it themselves.

JOHN SALADINO

A *new ruralist pioneer*. Way back in the sixties, he was juxtaposing ancient plaster walls with sleekly modern stainless steel ceilings.

ROUGH-LUXE

The term coined for new ruralists' favorite style — *half rough and half luxe*. Four star amenities and materials surrounded by the stately decadence of decay.

ARTISANAL

Hand-made. Hand-wrought. Woven. *Crafted*. Mass-produced need not apply.

Mirrors are custom-made to seem "crusty and old" and curtains are crisp oyster-color silk from J. Robert Scott.

" I will always be inspired when I see a photo of an Axel Vervoordt piece, where he's taken an old discarded thing and transformed it into something beautiful. I found those planters covered with moss and I turned them upside down to make platforms for candles in front of the mirrors. It's magic."
—KAY DOUGLASS, DESIGNER

THE TRADITIONALIST WITH A TWIST

If you had a time machine you'd love to travel to the past—but only for design inspiration! Covering a classic Chippendale sofa in an overblown damask or loosening up your oh-so-formal dining room with outsized black-and-white stripes is your kind of "traditional." You're all about familiar silhouettes that are full of surprises.

YOUR STYLE, DEFINED
Of-the-moment but rooted firmly in tradition and history. Civilized, polished, refined, cultured, polite but never ever proper.

MUST-HAVES
Antiques/family heirlooms, Oriental carpets, portraiture, wingchairs, symmetry, tufting, and monograms on every bath towel.

GO-TO BLOGS
grantgibson.blogspot.com
mrsblandings.blogspot.com
thedevinelife.blogspot.com
thepeakofchic.blogspot.com

A FEW TRADITIONALIST OBSESSIONS

1. **San Marco wallpaper** from China Seas through Quadrille
2. **Chippendale** from Ethan Allen
3. **Key tray** from Christofle
4. **Ispahan Birds tile** from Country Floors
5. **Roman Villa** thank you cards from Bell'Invito
6. **Spencer Lamp** by Michael S. Smith through Circa Lighting

TRADITIONALIST
Glossary

MARIO BUATTA

The designer who single-handedly American-ized the *English Country look*. "The prince of chintz" has been triumphantly upholster-ing sofas, chaises, even walls, in cabbage roses and ribbons since 1963.

NANCY LANCASTER

The mother of all traditionalists. Longtime owner of fabric house *Colefax & Fowler* and designer of the iconic Yellow Room at Avery Row, Mayfair.

PRE-WAR

The good old days for traditionalists, when houses had *formal dining rooms* and their denizens "dressed" for dinner.

TOILE DE JOUY

Fabric patterns with pastoral scenes like this one from *Pierre Frey* date back to 16th-century France — an example of what traditionalists mean when they say Old World (see below).

THE ENGLISH COUNTRYSIDE

A traditionalist paradise teem-ing with mahogany sideboards, Windsor chairs and *oil portraits* of long-departed hunting dogs.

OLD WORLD

Anything traditionalists speak about reverentially that can remotely be traced back to a *European design* tradition (see above).

A trio of 1950s Venetian de Majo chandeliers hangs over the Jacobean-style refectory table. The mix of patterned textiles includes Bennison's Pandaranda on the banquette, Nobilis's Manoir in Pale Blue on painted Louis XV–style chairs.

"A home to me is a living breathing thing. It's like your children. It has its own identity. That identity is built over time."
—ALESSANDRA BRANCA, DESIGNER

THE MODERNIST

Don Draper could walk into your place and head straight for the martini shaker. When you visit New York your first stop is the Seagram Building. Second stop, Lever House. Third stop, the MoMA. Tchotchkes are the bane of your existence. Sleek furniture lines and swathes of solid color ring your bell. Just the suggestion of a Victorian B&B weekend gives you nightmares.

YOUR STYLE, DEFINED
Uber-today with a dash of old-school minimalism—sleek, crisp, clean, impeccable, pristine. And, numero uno— no clutter, ever.

MUST-HAVES
Lucite, concrete, stainless steel, architectural brio, bleached leather, hide rugs, Noguchi lamps and somewhere, always, a Saarinen table.

GO-TO BLOGS
carolinaeclectic.blogspot.com
contemporist.com
mocoloco.com

A FEW MODERNIST OBSESSIONS

1. **Malhoun** by Didier Gomez through Ligne Roset

2. *Jean-Michel Frank* by Pierre-Emmanuel Martin-Vivier

3. **Lacquer Nesting Cubes** from Jonathan Adler

4. **Diva vase** from Baccarat

5. **Rock crystal lamp,** Carved Ice through McGuire Furniture

6. **Orange Leather Framed Mirror** by Made Goods through Mecox Gardens

MODERNIST
Glossary

JOHN PAWSON

An English architect/ designer currently showing the world the power of *rigorous minimalism*.

FARNSWORTH HOUSE

A 1951 *Mies van der Rohe* house in Plano, Illinois, so supernaturally pure, simplified and uncluttered it's become a modernist shrine.

BILLY BALDWIN

A mid-century modernist god whose furniture was *pared down*, tailored and, like his favorite chair (Billy Baldwin slipper chair pictured), also quite comfy.

REDUCTIVE

In the modernist bible every design element is reductive—low-key mantels, barely there moldings, *understated* statement pieces.

URBANE

The adjective modernists live for: smooth, slick, polished but with a certain *irresistible* charm.

ZEN

The definition of a successful modernist space—always *meditation–ready*.

"I love the way concrete floors look—so clean and smooth. They're the color of wet sand, and cool to bare feet. I like to subvert expectations by using industrial materials in a high-end setting."
—VICENTE WOLF, DESIGNER

The resin-topped dining table is surrounded by Philippe Starck's Louis Ghost chairs and Texstyle's Tub chairs upholstered in lime-green linen with leather seat cushions.

THE ACCESSORATOR

For you, decorating is a buffet and your plate is never big enough. You've got a "don't fence me in" view of design—there are too many beautiful things in the world to limit yourself to a single style. Vacations mean bringing home more bags than you left with and an urgent need to make room for that something new and fabulous.

YOUR STYLE, DEFINED

Happy, flirty and fresh. Lots of color, a keen eye for fashion, an enthusiastic just-gotta-have-it shopping M.O. You've never met a style that didn't mix.

MUST-HAVES

Anything pink, Greek key borders, wicker, painted screens, trellises, lacquer, flower prints.

GO-TO BLOGS

accessorator.com
delightbydesign.blogspot.com
stylecourt.blogspot.com
emilyevanseerdmans.blogspot.com
ohjoy.blogs.com/my_weblog

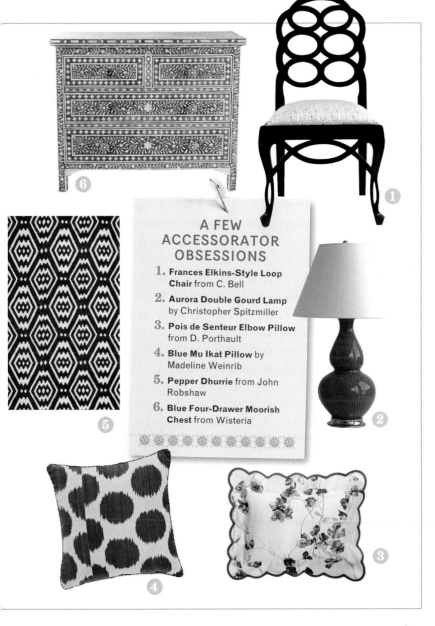

A FEW ACCESSORATOR OBSESSIONS

1. **Frances Elkins-Style Loop Chair** from C. Bell

2. **Aurora Double Gourd Lamp** by Christopher Spitzmiller

3. **Pois de Senteur Elbow Pillow** from D. Porthault

4. **Blue Mu Ikat Pillow** by Madeline Weinrib

5. **Pepper Dhurrie** from John Robshaw

6. **Blue Four-Drawer Moorish Chest** from Wisteria

ACCESSORATOR
Glossary

FOO DOG STATUES
Originally created as guardians of Chinese Buddhist temples, now a *favorite* of accessorators.

PARIS FLEAS
Not the ones on the stray *chiens*. The *flea markets of Paris* are the ultimate destination— acres of second-hand brio just begging for a new home… yours.

CONTROLLED CLUTTER
Maybe not always *"controlled"* but that's what they call it anyway.

DAVID HICKS
The late English designer is the unchallenged accessorator guru. His fabrics, wallpaper and rugs are *runaway bestsellers* with this crowd.

SUPER-CUTE
A word invented by accessorators as the *highest* possible compliment.

MADELINE CASTAING
So what if she held her wig on with an elastic chinstrap? She was the *queen of accessories* and her Paris shop was a zany mecca for designers. Even taxidermy and plastic flowers became beautiful as they passed through her chic little hands.

> **"I'm all for lots of accessories—they keep your eye moving around. My style of decorating is, 'I love this, I love that, let's put it all together and make it work.'"**
> **—KRISTA EWART, DESIGNER**

A vintage coffee table and stool in Hable Construction's Sweet Pea Beads sit on a zebra-print rug by Jonathan Adler.

1 | GLAM

A nervy mix of everything
from gilt to statuary, set off
by bold brave color

LEFT: "'Exuberantly
Feminine, Yet Resolutely
Chic.' That became
our motto."
—JONATHAN BERGER,
DESIGNER

The hand-painted wall-
paper is by de Gournay.
A pair of chairs, painted
chalky milk white, are
covered in Scalamandré's
Anemone.

OPPOSITE: "Pink was our
main statement, and we
used bits of it throughout
the house, taming it with
browns, pale blues, and
creams," says Berger.
An Italian gilt-brass
game table is surrounded
by chairs covered in
pink leather from
Global Leathers.

ENTRYWAYS

EXUBERANT | LAVISH | UNBRIDLED

"I came across an amazing design on an 18th-century Swedish wallpaper. I loved the big bold pattern, the movement. I adapted it for the artist who painted it onto these walls. You have those vines rising into the air, so it gives you a bit of an ethereal feeling." —TIMOTHY WHEALON, DESIGNER

Whealon extended the alfresco theme with a green lacquer David Hicks garden seat and lattice-motif Madeline Weinrib Brooke rug in Chocolate. Chairs are covered in Claudine in Chocolate by Les Indiennes.

OPPOSITE: A variation on a classic de Gournay wallpaper was made for the foyer. The neoclassical console and faux-malachite column lamps are from John Rosselli. Redd stained the floor's chevron pattern in contrasting tones to play up its geometry.

"My clients wanted you to walk into a wow factor. It's more typically seen in dining rooms or bedrooms than in entrance halls. So to immediately enter into a mad hand-painted garden scene—it's fresh." —MILES REDD, DESIGNER

ENTRYWAYS

....

PLUSH FURNITURE AND RICH COLORS
ARE ALWAYS WELCOME SURPRISES

"A friend said, 'I don't get it.
How can an eggplant sofa
work in a robin's-egg–blue
room with cherry-red curtains
and lemon-yellow slipcovers?'
They simply do. They
assist each other."
—JEFFREY BILHUBER, DESIGNER

A "stoic and imposing" entrance hall didn't appeal to Bilhuber. Instead, he created a reception hall that is all about hospitality and comfort. Sea green, sky blue, deep purple and lemon yellow make a happy combination of colors. Walls are covered in Celtic Square from Carleton V. China matting from Beauvais contrasts with black-painted pine floor planks.

"I love the spontaneous combinations of furniture and objects."

LIVING ROOMS

"I love that saffron-y silk velvet on the chair with the arched back, and wanted to do something on the walls that would really set it off. That's how I came up with the pink. It's fresh and exciting. The sofa is covered with a blue embroidered bedspread. I collect and collect, then lay it all out and see how these eclectic bits come together." —WINDSOR SMITH, DESIGNER

The Regency-style Samantha Scroll Arm Chair, upholstered in Pisanello silk velvet from Scalamandré, is from Smith's furniture line. The walls are painted Benjamin Moore Pink Begonia, with Decorators White on the trim.

"I learned all about scale in my twenty-two years working with **Albert Hadley**. In a high-ceilinged room, it's exciting to feel the height. That's why I used the pedestals with the urns in the windows—it makes you notice the height of the window."
—**BUNNY WILLIAMS, DESIGNER**

The sofa is in solid velvet, so patterned throws and pillows can easily change its look. Walls are painted Benjamin Moore California Breeze. Curtains made of Indian bedspreads frame an urn from John Rosselli Antiques & Decorations. Leather edges and a lift-out tray let the Tray Chic Ottoman multitask as table, bench, and footstool.

COLOR CONSULTATION

LIVING ROOMS WRAPPED IN OUTRAGEOUS COLOR ARE PURE GLAM. DESIGNERS CHOOSE SOME OF THEIR FAVORITE HUES.

JOE NYE FEELS GOOD INSIDE A ROOM PAINTED FARROW & BALL BABOUCHE 223

"This is a crazy combination of canary yellow, citron, and a little egg yolk all rolled into one. It's a feel-good color, because it's light and refreshing and bright. I did a room in it, with a ton of wicker furniture painted spinach green and covered in a multicolored chintz."

MILES REDD CREATES AN EMERALD GLOW WITH BENJAMIN MOORE AMAZON MOSS 2037-10

"This is the color of the felt on the billiards table in a Merchant Ivory film—all intense and glowy. There's something modern and old-fashioned about it at the same time. It's like being submerged into the center of a 40-carat emerald."

WILLIAM DIAMOND IS WILD ABOUT MARTIN-SENOUR MARINE GREEN 152-3

"How do you describe this? It's a Dorothy Draper color, somewhere between turquoise and chartreuse, the wildest color you've ever seen."

PINK WALLS PROVIDE A BUDDING BURST OF GLAM

"Pink is always on my mind. I just have to find a taker. This client couldn't be happier with her cheery pink sitting room. This pink, Benjamin Moore Coral Pink, is completely unexpected—it's the color of borscht with cream. It's like a cherry in your drink." —MARY McDONALD

LIVING ROOMS

ORANGE WARMS A ROOM WITH
GRAND PROPORTIONS

"You tame strong color by adding a lot of neutrals—woods, browns, beiges, creams, golds, silvers. I have no idea what you'd call this wall color, but it mixes easily with the spotted rug, the tiger silk throw, and the African masks, which lend a certain chic, exotic element to the room."
—NED MARSHALL, DESIGNER

Warm orange lends "a cozy feel to what is a rather cold space." He blended Benjamin Moore paints to get just the right color, which was inspired by the Hermès-box orange leather of the Louis XV–style armchairs.

"This is a large room with 14-foot ceilings, but I wanted it to be a cozy room for cocktails, so a warm color was really imperative. I designed the room around four orange leather-covered Louis XV–style fauteuils."

LIVING ROOMS

....

Walls are lacquered in Farrow & Ball
Hague Blue, "a great way to do a moody
color because of the way it reflects light.
It doesn't look dark so much as rich."
The mix of chairs includes Maison Jansen
slipper chairs upholstered in Velours de
Soie Uni in Bleu de France from Prelle.

"I love all colors, but I really love jewel
tones. The low slipper chairs have
peacock-blue silk velvet, which isn't
exactly the color of the walls but works
with them in an offbeat way. Walls are
lacquered; they have the quality of light
of a Vermeer painting and I like them
juxtaposed with rougher things—like
the orange felt-covered console."
—MILES REDD, DESIGNER

"It was just a white box when we moved in. We added moldings, antique doors, window niches, and the wood floor for character. And there's a density of color here that makes it feel enveloping and warm instead of pinched and anemic. It sort of wraps around you." —DAVID KAIHOI, DESIGNER

To open up floor space in his living room Kaihoi built a corner banquette, covered in purple velvet from Elegant Fabrics. Zebra pillows are in Tigre Velours Soie from Clarence House. Walls are painted Benjamin Moore Purple Haze.

DESIGNER
Master class

How would
you glam up a
simple classic
armchair like the
TYLER ARMCHAIR
from Oly?

"This chair can slip in anywhere.
The challenge is to keep it from
looking too pedestrian. I'd give
it two different attitudes. The
front, in leather, is masculine,
contemporary. The back, in
floral, is feminine, whimsical.
I'd put bronze nailheads on top
of blue grosgrain and paint the
frame white in a flat finish."

—WINDSOR SMITH

BARRINGTON LEATHER IN QUARTZ:
MOOREANDGILESINC.COM. ALL
OVER FLORAL NEGATIVE PALE GREY
ON OYSTER: BENISON FABRICS.COM.
GROSGRAIN IN COLOR 287: HYMANHENDLER.COM.
HARDWICK WHITE PAINT NO. 5: FARROW-BALL.COM.

"You can be adventurous with a chair, unlike a sofa. Red is happening again! This fabric is wildly graphic, but in a polished way. I'd trim it with a ruby leather braid and use red lacquer nailheads. And red raffia on the back, accented with an X in a ruby-and-black band. To play up the silhouette, lacquer it black."

—LARRY LASLO

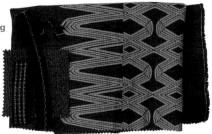

METROPOLE IN HABANERO, MAR A LAGO IN ROJO, ALCHEMY LEATHER AND BAND BY LARRY LASLO: ROBERTALLENDESIGN.COM. BLACK MAGIC PAINT SW 6991: SHERWIN-WILLIAMS.COM.

"I really like this French-style chair— it's a classic. But I'd make it more hip, more rock 'n' roll—a conversation piece. People love dogs! You don't need to center them, but there should be one or two full dogs somewhere—no little behinds on the edges! Use French natural finish nailheads and paint the chair metallic gold to add a little flash."

—BARCLAY BUTERA

KINGSLEY IN DAPPLE BY BARCLAY BUTERA: KRAVET.COM. CHAMPAGNE TOAST PAINT, RM 33: RALPHLAURENHOME.COM.

"Oly's Tyler chair has a great form, and it's well priced. I use it a lot. I chose a faux snakeskin in melon—smashing!—even wrapping it all around the seat frame. I'd embellish the base with polished brass nailheads in a zigzag pattern, and add polished brass cuffs to the feet to give the legs more dimension."

—PAT HEALING

PRISMATEK'S PITON IN COLOR 37 BY FINE EUROPEAN FABRIC: FSCHUMACHER.COM. 1⅜" POLISHED BRASS SQUARE CUP SOCKET: WHITECHAPEL-LTD.COM

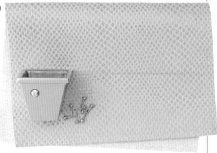

STYLE SEMINAR
with Suzanne Tucker

This San Francisco designer was once the protégé of the legendary designer Michael Taylor. Following in his footsteps, her favorites are glam to the max.

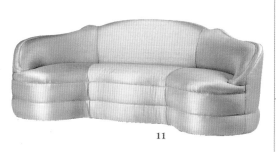

11

16

17

1. **All-purpose Glass:** Crate & Barrel Bistro glass

2. **Artist:** Mark Rothko

3. **Bed Pillow:** 100% down, light fill with Léron pillowcases

4. **Car Color** (exterior/interior): Black/camel leather

5. **Coffee Table Book:** *Michael Taylor: Interior Design* by Stephen M. Salny (www.norton.com)

6. **Coffee or Tea:** Peet's dark French Roast in the morning, Fortnum & Mason Royal Blend Tea in the afternoon

7. **Color:** Shooting Star, Benjamin Moore #304

8. **Comfort Food:** Dark chocolate

9. **Stationery:** Mrs. John L. Strong anything

10. **Everyday Dishes:** Williams-Sonoma white with textured border. Thin, not clunky

11. **Sofa Shape:** Schiaparelli—custom-made or through Michael Taylor Designs

12. **Lamp:** Rock crystal anything!

13. **Lightbulb/Wattage:** Soft white 60W

14. **Mattress:** McRoskey Mattress

15. **Picture Frame:** Tiffany Baby Birth Record Frame

16. **Soap:** Annick Goutal's Eau d'Hadrien

17. **Flower:** Pink peony

18. **Wallpaper:** Farrow & Ball dragged paper, #BP6lt

19. **Workhorse Fabric:** Marvic Woven Chenille

18th-century Venetian mirrors, found by Michael Taylor, hang above consoles copied from a console formerly in Taylor's own entry hall.

"This house was originally done by Michael Taylor in 1979. The clients wanted to warm up the living room. So I painted the walls a pale apricot. Then I stood in the space and thought, what would Michael do now? So I reupholstered the furniture in stone and tobacco. If the fabric didn't have texture, I added it with quilting. Michael loved quilting and crewel." —SUZANNE TUCKER

LIVING ROOMS

SHOTS OF GILT AND GOLD LEND
GLAMOUR TO A NEUTRAL PALETTE.

"Over the mantel I've placed the most unique religious object that I own. It's a beautiful old gilt piece, and I don't know the proper name for it but I call it a sacrament plaque. All those individual slots have places to put a name, and as you received your sacrament, they would add your name. It was from a small neighborhood church somewhere in France."

"At heart, I'm a modernist. I begin with modern bones. But I still love antiquity—a beautiful reliquary or a great old gilt piece."
—NANCY PRICE
   DESIGNER

....

"I'm wildly intrigued with religious art. I went to St. Rita Catholic School in Louisiana, and we were required to go to Mass three times a week. I always stared at Mary in her blue cloak. How I loved those statues!"

....

"The rectilinear leather chaise and sleek cylindrical stone side table are clear modernist statements. But the mantelpiece, ornamented with a reliquary, sacrament plaque, chipped blue-robed statue, and crowns reveals a passion for ornate gilt antiques."

Tablescape

Silk Organza Napkin from Kim Seybert

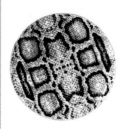

Snakeskin from Kiln Enamel

Large Mint Julep Cup from Lexington Gardens

Spring Lark dinnerware from Marchesa by Lenox

Paisley Bloom stemware from Marchesa by Lenox

Escot in green from William Yeoward Crystal

"If you want to inject your party with glamour, dress up! Your table should dress the part, too. You don't have to overdo it—even a small gesture like tucking a flower bud into each napkin can add a touch of couture elegance to any setting."
—GEORGINA CHAPMAN AND KEREN CRAIG, FOUNDERS OF THE FASHION HOUSE MARCHESA

Palatial Garden dinnerware by Marchesa for Lenox; ice bucket, turquoise charger, and bud vases by Lenox.

DINING ROOMS

"While we were decorating, the homeowner and I went to France. We brought back the mood. This wallpaper is a modern toile by Pierre Frey. The sconces are French Art Deco but the dining chairs are from Crate & Barrel. They're upholstered in ivory linen, and we tweaked them by having the company pipe them in chocolate brown." —STEPHEN SHUBEL, DESIGNER

Wallpaper is Pierre Frey's Sintra wallpaper in Tournesol. "I added cowhide rugs so it didn't feel too precious and pretty," says Shubel. Crate & Barrel dining chairs are mixed with a pair of 1820s Biedermeier chairs upholstered in cognac silk velvet from Old World Weavers. The curtains are Dedar's Leonia silk in Dore.

"I'd been wanting to use that silver tea paper for a long time— it brings such a warm luminescence into a room. Then the rug is a wonderful juxtaposition, a perfect foil for the formality and fanciness of the Gracie paper. And I've always been fond of that faux bois moiré print on the chairs. It's elegant and earthy at the same time." —ANDREW RAQUET, DESIGNER

The striped wool Venetian carpet from Thistle Hill Weavers "keeps the room from being too precious." Chairs are covered in Alan Campbell's Meloire Reverse. The silver tea-leaf wallpaper is from Gracie.

Sparklers

Trillion Flushmount from Visual Comfort

Elizabeth Five Arm Chandelier from Paris Market & Brocante

Abalone, Selected Works of Tony Duquette from Baker Furniture

Meurice from Jonathan Adler

Monaco from Niermann Weeks

"That huge Venetian chandelier has a glow that's like looking through a glass of champagne—especially after you've had a few glasses yourself. It goes with those Queen Anne-ish chairs that are sort of Syrie Maugham by way of Samuel Marx."
—JOE NAHEM, DESIGNER

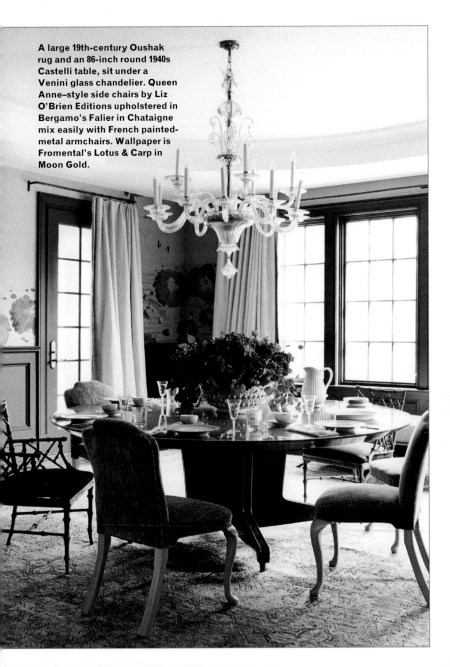

A large 19th-century Oushak rug and an 86-inch round 1940s Castelli table, sit under a Venini glass chandelier. Queen Anne–style side chairs by Liz O'Brien Editions upholstered in Bergamo's Falier in Chataigne mix easily with French painted-metal armchairs. Wallpaper is Fromental's Lotus & Carp in Moon Gold.

DINING ROOMS

BOLD DINING CHAIRS CREATE FULL-ON IMPACT

"The furniture is rather curvaceous. It has a softening effect on the rectilinear architecture. Most people aren't fearless enough. The reason there are so many bland interiors is that people are scared." —JAMIE DRAKE, DESIGNER

Chairs from Artistic Frame have seats in Larsen patent leather. Curtains in the dining area are in Drake's Jazzed for Schumacher, a cotton whose stripes alternate between matte and sateen. The painting is by Irene Mamiye.

"The dining room was so
architecturally spare, I
decided to introduce a touch
of exoticism to the furnishings. The fabric on the dining
chairs is a reinterpretation of
a Suzani pattern, and it was
the pattern that dictated the
shape of the chairs. It had to
lay out a certain way."
—JEFFREY BILHUBER,
   DESIGNER

Chairs, covered in Donghia's Suzani
Jacquard in Blue Bliss, are paired with a
round English Regency–style table and a
curved banquette upholstered in Cowtan
& Tout's Lucerne in yellow. The 1960s
French chandelier is from Amy Perlin.

KITCHENS

....

LUSCIOUS | RICH | SPICY

"The kitchen existed. It had a good-quality laminate and I thought, why replace this with a paneled kitchen? I knew it would paint beautifully—and that a strong brush of color would make it exciting. I kept thinking: British racing green, the color of a 1962 Jag. But that turned out to be too dark. So we pumped up the color just a scootch and lacquered it to give it life." —**MILES REDD, DESIGNER**

The small kitchen's cabinets are lacquered in **Bamboo Leaf** by **Fine Paints of Europe**, as was the roller shade by **Manhattan Shade & Glass**, which erases an exhaust unit. Even the **Sub-Zero** refrigerator is painted green.

"The banana leaf wallpaper is a great continuation of the courtyard just outside the doors, and the fun feeling of it seems appropriate here in New Orleans with all its tropical humidity." —HAL WILLIAMSON, DESIGNER

Life-size banana leaves—the **Beverly Hills Hotel** signature wallpaper—lends drama to a small kitchen.

COLOR CONSULTATION

COLOR IN THE KITCHEN IS A GLAM MUST-DO:
DESIGNERS CHOOSE SOME OF THEIR FAVORITE HUES

MARK CUTLER RIFFS ON A FAMOUS PARIS PATISSERIE
WITH FINE PAINTS OF EUROPE P11130

"I have one of those little green boxes from Ladurée, that Paris pastry shop, on my desk. Turns out my client has one, too, and we re-created that Ladurée green on her kitchen island. It's an incredibly complex color, a weird combination of yellow and green with this red undertone. Beautiful."

PHILIP GORRIVAN IS MAGNETIZED BY BENJAMIN MOORE
RAZZLE DAZZLE 1348

"Pick one wall. Apply two coats of Rust-Oleum Magnetic primer, paint it this yummy raspberry color, and then put up your children's artwork, school schedules, and birthday invites with magnets."

ERICA BROBERG TURBOCHARGES A KITCHEN WITH
BENJAMIN MOORE MERLOT RED 2006-10

"Red is energizing, invigorating, and this is the perfect red, not too orange and not too blue. It works equally well in sunny or dark rooms and really sets off the cabinets, which we order primed, and then paint on-site with a nice brushed finish."

TURQUOISE ADDS A CONFIDENT DOSE OF CHIC TO A HOMEY KITCHEN
"The work island is absolutely as creative and stylish as we could make it.
It's made of powder-coated steel with mirror-finish stainless steel trim. And
we covered the kitchen ceiling in our Harlequin wallpaper. Then the floor was
stenciled with lemons and limes." —**WILLIAM DIAMOND**

KITCHENS

MIRRORS IN THE KITCHEN? WHY NOT?

"When the architect suggested lattice on the walls, I came up with the idea
of laying antiqued mercury glass mirror behind it. The lattice itself gives the
room a garden feel, and the reflection brings the outdoors in."
—ALLISON CACCOMA, DESIGNER

Louis XV–style chairs are covered in Robert Kime's Tashkent. Paul Ferrante's
Gardner fixture hangs over the David Iatesta Provençale dining table. Both are
from John Rosselli.

"We got the idea to make our kitchen look like a beautiful dining room. The stove is like a sideboard. Don't dining rooms always have big mirrors over the sideboard? Opposite the stove there's a big bay window overlooking the garden. You can look up while you're cooking and see all the greenery."
—RICHARD NORRIS, DESIGNER

The hub of the house is also its dressiest room. Over the Five Star stove is a silver-leaf Napoleon III mirror. The chandelier was fashioned from a pair of antique bronze sconces.

What's the most glamorous thing you've done lately?

"I am loving my new Dornbracht kitchen faucet— the Elio Single-level mixer in brushed nickel. It looks like a beautiful sculpture, as if modern geometric design had somehow converged with a swan's neck. What I love most: It adds so much style to an otherwise not-very-interesting place in my apartment."
—PHILIP GORRIVAN

"I recently did a design job in a very contemporary house. In the entry, I put a beautiful Louis XVI table gilded in 22-karat gold, with a marble top. It was the only traditional thing in the whole house and it stood out like a piece of jewelry. It was just so noticeable, floating on this marble space with lots of light."
—NANCY CORZINE

"Sit down. Take a swallow. In my living room I have a pair of doors covered in zebra hides and detailed with silver nailheads. The play of stripes is so arresting."
—MILES REDD

"First, I took down the curtains in my bedroom and lacquered the walls a sexy tan color. Then I made my own moldings with tortoiseshell bamboo—split lengthwise so it lies flat. I used it to outline the windows and the doors and the tray ceiling. Handsome and tropical."
—BROOKE HUTTIG

"I draped a Mongolian lamb's wool throw over my lumpy old sofa and suddenly it was luxurious and exotic."
—DAVID MANN

Slim Chaise, covered in Kravet's Obsession, and Zebra Bed from Windsor Smith Home.

"I found this amazing embroidered satin from Bergamo Fabrics and used it on the bed to create a little jewel box. And then I added that whimsical Italian mirror. It's like a star hanging over us." —WINDSOR SMITH

BEDROOMS

"My client saw a picture of this bed (it's my own bed—designed by the famous French firm Jansen) and loved it, and the mirror man said he could copy it. By the time he finished it, he swore he'd *never* do that again."
—**BUNNY WILLIAMS, DESIGNER**

The wall-hanging behind the dazzling mirrored bed—dressed in **Pratesi** sheets—was embroidered in India. A silvery blue-gray silk carpet was found at **Beauvais**.

"We made a few risky moves, but we're glad we did. Lavender is my client's favorite color, and she knew from the start that she wanted a lavender bedroom. She told me the other day that this would have been her dream room when she was growing up. Even her husband likes it! It's restful, romantic, and happy."
—ANDREW RAQUET, DESIGNER

Cheverny by Manuel Canovas covers the headboard and outer layer of the bed curtain, lined in Lane Stripe by Quadrille. The silvery moiré wallcovering is by Robert Crowder. *Faux-marbre* painting on bedside table by Mary Kuzma Finishing. Leontine Linens.

STYLE SEMINAR
with Mary McDonald

| This Los Angeles–based designer isn't afraid of anything—not even a tented bedroom. Follow her lead to create an ultra-glam bedroom of your own.

TENT THE WHOLE ROOM IN A RAW SILK IKAT! THEN PAPER THE WALLS IN SUBTLE TEXTURE.

"Kazak (in orange/pink) from Quadrille is deliciously summery. When you're surrounded by it, you can't help but feel happy. I like a layer of mystery under the tenting. Pull back the curtains and you can really see this paper—Japanese paper weave (in Palm) from Phillip Jeffries."

MAKE A HEADBOARD AND SLIPPER CHAIRS THAT ARE BRIGHT FOCAL POINTS.

"Molucca (in orange) from Fonthill is casual but vibrant, a fantastic orange."

TRIM HOT-PINK THROW PILLOWS IN ALL THE COLORS OF THE ROOM.

"Shabby (in Tyrien) from Pierre Frey is perfect for throw pillows because it has such great woven texture. I'd trim pillows with Cabana Braid (in coral) from Schumacher. It matches all the colors so well, it looks custom!"

GLAM UP SLIPPER CHAIRS WITH WOOD-FRINGE BEADS AND A DOUBLE BORDER.

"I do a double border often. I like the tailored, graphic look of Rustic Naturals Border with Plaited Border from Ralph Lauren Home. And, oh the summery madness of wood-fringed beads! Maasai Beaded Grass Fringe from Samuel & Sons is sort of Madeleine Castaing at the beach."

TREAT X-BENCHES TO FAUX-BOIS MADNESS.

"Meloire Reverse (in orange) from Quadrille is a playful take on faux-bois. I thought the room needed a few patterns that wouldn't compete with the all-encompassing tent fabric."

COVER A BENCH IN A MODERN PRINT FOR BALANCE.

"Saya Gata (in orange) through Quadrille is modern and it mixes well with the old-school–inspired ikat. The simpler pattern helps create balance in the room."

BEDROOMS

WAKING UP IN AN ALL-RED ROOM IS
ABOUT AS GLAM AS A DAY CAN GET

"When I did my bedroom, I had in mind *Brideshead Revisited*, and that defining
moment when Lord Marchmain lies in his bed receiving family and friends.
His room was big and light and it opened onto the garden: It gave me great
comfort." —JEFFREY BILHUBER, DESIGNER

With tongue-in-cheek ingenuity, Bilhuber attached valances and curtain rods
to a wooden frame on the ceiling to conjure up the illusion of a palatial tester
bed. Damask is Cote Bosque by Owens & Perry.

Schumacher stripes and graphics, vintage florals, and a Bergamo rug from Asmara. The green wall is Benjamin Moore Chamomile. Asian nesting tables were custom-made by Mary McDonald. Chinese Chippendale bench from Out of Asia.

"People have rules about bedrooms, that they're always supposed to be soft and pastel. Why can't they be zippy and vibrant?"—MARY McDONALD, DESIGNER

"The bedroom has these faux-ivory walls painted in a delicate grid pattern with faux-horn trim—a very modern Taj Mahal. You feel you're in a cool ivory box."
—MILES REDD, DESIGNER

Rough textures play up the silky walls in the master bedroom. Redd discovered the convex mirror framed with crude antique oak at Treillage and found a place for it over the headboard. It's covered in Edelman Royal Suede in pitch brown. Bedside lamps are by John Saladino. The Cubist dhurrie rug is from Vaughan. Curtains are Brunschwig & Fils' Bankers Linen in Scarlet.

"The wallpaper is 18th-century Chinese. I stumbled across it at an auction, this pile of dilapidated pieces that nobody else wanted. I found three large scenes, placed them around the room, and pieced in the gaps and torn bits. The idea was to distract your senses from the tight quarters."
—DAVID KAIHOI, DESIGNER

"The trundle bed for our daughter only comes out at night and gets pushed back under the bed first thing in the morning," Kaihoi says. They use the windowsill in the 64-square-foot room as their bedside table.

BATHROOMS

"The settee is French, from the 1930s. I love it there. It's so finely carved, and the gilt is so reflective of the light. We kept the original cushion because it was obviously tufted by hand. Exquisite! It makes the bathroom look dressed up. I think people should furnish a bath just as they would any other room in the house." —CARRIE HAYDEN, DESIGNER

The settee adds a graceful silhouette: "Just because there are polished nickel faucets doesn't mean you can't also have gilt. The nickel pieces are functional, the gold pieces are accents—they don't have to match."

A vanity table links a pair of mirrored bureaus fitted with sinks. Thick slabs
of honed Calacatta marble for backsplashes and counters, along with Waterworks Opus faucets and an antique gilt mirror complete the dressy old-world
European feeling.

"That vanity is actually made from two dressers that were in the bedroom of the
homeowners. I created the sit-down bridge in between for even more glamour.
The vanity sconces have crystal arms, and the sink faucets have crystal handles. The ambient light at night is beautiful, reflecting off the gold and crystal."
—CARRIE HAYDEN

CHAPTER 2

NEW RURALIST

Natural materials play against the soulful patina of aged antiques and Mother Nature's perfect hues

LEFT: **"This style is a blend of our interests in both humble, rustic houses and turn-of-the-century industrial-style warehouses. It's part farmhouse, part loft." — JILL SHARP BRINSON, DESIGNER**

OPPOSITE: **The beams in this renovated Atlanta cottage are salvaged from North Carolina tobacco barns. "I'm a huge no-color girl. Oyster shell and steel gray with a lot of truffle, that's my palette," says Brinson.**

ENTRYWAYS

LUMINOUS | UNPRETENTIOUS | WELCOMING

"I aim for a harmony of opposites. Ancient and modern, shiny and matte, primitive and civilized, serious and witty." — BETSY BROWN, DESIGNER

A Dutch ebony and brass mirror hangs above an unusual antique turned gate-leg table. Floors are reclaimed oak floors, bleached and limed.

"See that metal table in the entry? Did you notice that it's a little crooked, a little off? It has soul."
— JILL SHARP BRINSON, DESIGNER

A nine-foot-tall steel door replaced a wood door. The floor is reclaimed French limestone.

From a jumble
of hats to a
work of art.

"My client had a lot
of wonderful things
but they were so
cowboy-looking. He
had so many *objets* I
just wanted to white
everything out! This
way we accentuated
the positive and elimi-
nated the negative."
— **MYRA HOEFER,
DESIGNER**

HANDS OFF FOR FIRE USE ONLY

"I wanted it to be easy and livable. No precious materials. You don't worry about what's on your feet when you walk inside."
— KEN FULK, DESIGNER

Low-maintenance bluestone covers the floor and a salvaged fireman's rack became a coat rack in this Napa ranch house. Zebra-patterned ottoman is vintage.

LIVING ROOMS

ORGANIC | EARTHY | SOULFUL

A custom braided-wool rug warms the floor and a curly Mongolian lamb's wool covers an ottoman. Pillows are in Raoul Textiles's Secret Garden.

"The brown rings in the rug play off the brown woodwork of the walls and ceiling. Round rugs also make seating plans work in the way they're supposed to, forming circles of people. It's like extending arms, an invitation to literally gather round." —TOM SCHEERER, DESIGNER

The ceiling was stained dark and then washed with lichen-colored glaze.

"The wood is pecky cypress on the ceilings and clear cypress on the walls. A lot of pecky cypress is orange-toned, so we had to knock all the orange out to get the effect we wanted. I introduced green and gray into the stain on the floor, and that gave it a cooler tone, creating a sense of calm."
—SUSAN FERRIER, DESIGNER

COLOR CONSULTATION

A SIMPLE WHITE LIVING ROOM IS NEW RURALIST BLISS:
DESIGNERS CHOOSE SOME OF THEIR FAVORITES

MARIETTE HIMES GOMEZ IS A LOYAL FAN OF DONALD KAUFMAN 51

"This white is going to be with me for the rest of my life. You can see every color in it. It's a chameleon that changes with natural light. Anything you put near it is comfortable."

PETER PENNOYER MAKES IMPERFECTIONS PERFECT WITH FARROW & BALL STRONG WHITE

"If you have a wall with a bow in it or a floor that has settled, this will make an old room feel graceful rather than brand new. It has more pigment and therefore more character."

AMANDA MASTERS LIKES THE CLEAN LOOK OF RALPH LAUREN PAINT TIBETAN JASMINE WW37

"This is a soft white that opens up like a flower and makes a room look very clean, and it has this lovely antiqued or chalky quality that reminds me of lime-washed French bedrooms in summertime."

WHITE WALLS EXPAND A SPACE

"We boarded every wall with reclaimed wood and we whitewashed the boards
for warmth. And since rooms are small, I thought it was important to just enjoy
the architecture of the boards—not to close things up by using too much art."
— **GINGER BARBER, DESIGNER**

LIVING ROOMS

BELGIAN STYLE IS FRESH
AND FULL OF IMPACT

"It's okay if things look old and used.
And it's okay to keep things very very
simple. That's what I think this style—
Belgian style—is all about."
— KAY DOUGLASS, DESIGNER

"Slipcovers add
softness and
comfort to a room."

"The unstained light
wood console is
a typical Belgian
touch. The wood
tends to be lighter."

"I used neutral linens, many are Belgian linens, which are coarser, more natural. And I used color only to set a mood, not as a statement."

An unstained fireplace surround highlights the golden patina of natural wood. Walls are painted Benjamin Moore Seapearl. The sofa, in Perennials' Canvas Weave along with curtains in creamy linen from Lewis & Sheron present a neutral backdrop for wing chairs slipcovered in DeLany & Long's Seasand in Red.

STYLE SEMINAR
with Darryl Carter

This Washington, D.C.–based designer uses neutrals brilliantly. Follow his lead to create a New Ruralist living room of your own.

USE EMBROIDERY FOR CURTAINS
"Crewel on linen from Lee Jofa is weighty enough to drape perfectly, yet unstructured for more of a relaxed sensibility."

COVER A CHAIR IN BUTTERY LEATHER
"Superkidskin from Lee Jofa upholsters beautifully and mellows with wear, darkens and turns waxy. Think of a saddle."

MAKE A CRISP LINEN SOFA
"I like tailored upholstery. Trevin from Lee Jofa is lightweight, so it takes shape well. You get to see all the detail and architecture of the furniture."

DRESS A SMALL CHAIR IN BURLAP
"Powell Texture in Tan from Hinson is a very refined burlap. That's as natural as it gets!"

CHOOSE A NONCOMMITTAL COLOR FOR AN OTTOMAN
"I use Found from Lee Jofa in one of those neutral colors that's a bit noncommittal and lets you bring other colors into a room. It's just a wash of the palest blue with an undertone of faint apricot."

USE A SUBTLE PRINT FOR THROW PILLOWS
"Use Zilla from Malbar to introduce pattern into a room. It's a classic windowpane design, so it's likely to stand the test of time."

MAKE THROWS FROM LUXE WOOL
"Hush in Dove from Lee Jofa is an abstract, hushed paisley that will survive any trend."

UPHOLSTER THE WALLS IN LINEN!
"Ava in Sesame from Lee Jofa has a great middle weight and a mellow strié that's a natural part of the weave."

MANTELS—WHERE FOUND OBJECTS BECOME SCULPTURE

"I like wire. It lightens things up. I have wire-framed topiaries on the mantel and just in case you were wondering, that's an old wire parasol frame hanging behind them."
— ELLEN O'NEILL, DESIGNER

A pair of ebonized Parisian club chairs, á flea-market find, are perfectly scaled for a small room. The striped pillows are from Ikea. The wire café parasol frame above the fireplace is from Bloom.

The painting, *Gorgeous Grace*, is by Linda St. Clair.

"The limestone fireplace in the family room had an old Georgian wannabe mantel. We removed it and made this wonderful mantel shelf out of a simple old wood beam."
—GINGER BARBER, DESIGNER

The designers added the interior
shutters and painted the room
Pratt & Lambert Shadow Beige to
match the limestone fireplace.

"The shutters were made to order, and getting the color and weathered finish right almost defeated us. They look like they're peeling, and there are actual chunks of wood missing."
—KIM WINKLER, DESIGNER

....

"We wanted a pair of sofas that didn't look like the typical English roll-arms you see everywhere. These are low, sleek, and long—94 inches—and make an enormous impact when you walk through the front door."

....

"We're devoted to neutrals, to taupes, ivories, soft grays. Here, they're punched up with turquoise."

....

"There's a picture in Axel Vervoordt's book *Timeless Interiors* of one huge white slipcovered sofa with a low-slung coffee table, and it became our mantra on the project. We took all our cues from it."

INSPIRED OBSESSIONS

New Ruralist Tabletop

Christiane Perrochon through Urban Zen

Napoli linen napkin in Flax from Jayson Home & Garden

Elder II Candlestick from Lars Bolander

Egg Candles from MoMA Design Store

Mandara Bowl from Jayson Home & Garden

Sand Blasted Manzanita from Drynature

"You'll never make a mistake with a neutral table and all-white flowers. Wood, stone, water, flowers—being surrounded by nature is grounding for me." **—DONNA KARAN, FASHION DESIGNER**

DINING ROOMS

"That chandelier is lot of fun—the body is solid wood. I've never seen anything like it. Somebody doing a really formal dining room might say, 'Doesn't that look a bit, um, off-kilter?' But we thought a drunken chandelier looked right for a lake house." —SUSAN FERRIER, DESIGNER

The formal Louis XIII dining chairs are relaxed with a cowhide ottoman. A grid of tree prints repeats and balances the grid of the windows. The wood-and-iron chandelier is a French antique.

The Zettel'z 5 Chandelier by Ingo Maurer is made of love letters on Japanese paper. Hoefer designed the dining table in the style of a picnic table, and covered the backs of Patricia Edwards chairs with old army blankets.

"Northern California is very woody, it's like a sin to paint wood! Not for me. Paint it! Paint it white! The floor man was in shock. We did the floors in a high-gloss marine paint to give them some chic. The walls are a very pale gray. It's a color I created called Paris Gray. It has a light-ness to it." —MYRA HOEFER, DESIGNER

"**This house was originally a sea captain's house. By dumb luck, I came across a rare Currier & Ives print of Newport Harbor. I had it digitally enlarged, printed on canvas, and rolled onto the walls.**"
—**TOM SCHEERER, DESIGNER**

Leather cushions add height to a linen-covered Empire settee to match antique chairs pulled up to the custom table.

"We left the walls unfinished. The dining room is my real south-of-France moment. I wanted that 'old with the new' here. At night it feels so cavernous and cozy when you've got candles lit and they pick up the texture of the wall. It can be everything from austere to decadent."
—AMY NEUNSINGER, DESIGNER AND PHOTOGRAPHER

When turning the former master bath into the dining room, workers chipped away tiles to reveal a raw concrete wall creating "the ultimate old-world design moment." Pottery Barn chairs; Shabby Chic chandelier.

STYLE SEMINAR
with Peter Dunham

This L.A. designer always wows with his mash-ups of rustic and mod. His favorite things showcase the full New Ruralist experience.

4

6

1 | **7**

8

1. **Chair:** *How to Marry a Millionaire* from Hollywood at Home

2. **Alarm Clock:** Quadrono AB65 from Braun

3. **All–purpose Glass:** Ikea goblets, no stem, clear

4. **Wallpaper:** Fromental Chinese Sparrows, Shagreen, from fromental.co.uk

5. **Bed Pillow:** Tempurpedic neck pillow

6. **Everyday Dishes:** Coupe Line from Heath Ceramics

7. **Flower:** Sunflower

8. **Soap:** Santa Maria Novella

9. **Car Color** (exterior/interior): Silver/red

10. **Cleaning Supply:** Mrs. Meyer's Lavender

11. **Coffee or Tea:** Trader Joe's organic green tea

12. **Kitchen Gadget:** Nespresso

13. **Mattress:** Four Seasons

14. **Pen:** Sharpie ultra fine point in olive green

15. **Scented Candle or Room Fragrance:** Incenso & Ambra by L'Erbolario

16. **Sheets:** Deborah Sharpe Linens— ecru with custom Italian embroideries. 450–500 count

17. **Stationery:** Ivory with white-lined envelopes, from Tiffany

18. **Towel:** Waterworks Gotham in white/ecru, trimmed to match your bathroom

19. **Workhorse Fabric:** Hollister Linen from Hollywood at Home—natural color

Pillows are made from a vintage suzani from Design Utopia. Chairs are Dunham's signature *How to Marry a Millionaire* chairs.

"I thought of making two smaller tables and this overscale banquette. I wanted my client to be able to put the two dining tables together with the leaf in and feed a whole household. But he can also nestle in with one friend, or even lie down alone and watch television. This is my English side. We're big on creating destinations where we can nestle inside our drafty, cold, nasty houses."
— PETER DUNHAM

DINING ROOMS

BURNISHED, WELL AGED,
AND BARNYARD-CHIC

"I did three layers of white mixed with gray on the cabinets, and a spray-on lacquer finish."
—JILL SHARP BRINSON, DESIGNER

....

"My dining room looks a little mercantile. Like a cool dish shop in Sweden or France."

....

"I love seeing dishes through the chicken wire."

....

"If we have a dinner party, we just whisk the bench over and grab some weird little stools we have around."

....

Wicker chairs and white cowhide soften the industrial edge of the table, which extends another three feet. A Moroccan necklace drapes a bottle from **BoBo Intriguing Objects.**

DINING ROOMS

A DISTRESSED ÉTAGÈRE OR AN OPEN
ARMOIRE KEEP BEAUTIFUL THINGS IN THE LIGHT

The étagère is a workhorse—a place to set up a buffet, store dishes, display heirlooms, stack mail. Pounds designed the dining chairs. Tapestry is from Maison de France. Concrete tile flooring from Peacock Pavers.

"I do love exquisite things, like an antique linen napkin with a hand-stitched monogram. And if you come over for ribs, you can use one of those napkins."
—MELANIE POUNDS, DESIGNER

"You don't need to make a big fuss, just put together things that make you happy and that reflect you. I left the backs of chairs unfinished. The hand-tying is so beautiful, I thought 'Why cover it?' It makes me happy just to look at it. And it creates more texture in the room."
—DAN MARTY, DESIGNER

Marty ebonized the pine armoire and table to add depth, gloss, and contrast. The white pottery is part of his Astier de Villatte collection.

DESIGNER
Master class

" I actually had my own bathroom door fabricated recently. My metal guy cut simple, heavy plates of raw steel. Then he torched a rough design across the top—an Ethiopian cross. Light comes in through the cross. Now we call it the confessional. It has a rope handle that's knotted on both sides. Everyone who comes over says, 'I want those doors!'"

— ERIN MARTIN

" If you have a room paneled in new wood that is trying to look old, take a paintbrush and add a thin line of black in the flutes of a column, or along the raised part of a panel. That touch of black will add authenticity."

—TOM FLEMING

" With the hanging altar light I get from Holly Hunt. It looks like something you'd find in a church: a bronzed metal tray with a dozen or more oversize candles with embedded lightbulbs. We put them everywhere: over bathtubs, in dining rooms, in living rooms."

—LAURA BOHN

" Slipcover a sculptural chair in gauze. You'll see the form in shadow. Very intriguing."

—SUSAN FERRIER

Shelves
are painted
Benjamin
Moore South
Beach.

"Painting the inside of cabinets to add depth to what otherwise would be a blob of white. If the background were just white, the things in these cabinets wouldn't have any impact at all. They would have gotten lost." —JASON BELL

KITCHENS

DOWN-TO-EARTH | RICH | WARM

"The house wanted a big kitchen to be its symmetrical core, but that meant losing the dining room, so the kitchen had to be both."
—BETSY BROWN, DESIGNER

Limed-oak cabinets and Carrara marble counters. The 16-foot-long oak table was made by Tim Bell based on an Axel Vervoordt design. Painting by Guido Maus.

"I wanted something old and battered. Barn wood? Been there, done that. Then my cabinetmaker said he had a source for wood from a tobacco shed. I love that warm gray patina. It's very soulful."
—HILLARY HAYNE, DESIGNER

The table is made of 12-foot-long walnut planks. The vintage chrome chairs are upholstered in Brazilian cowhide. All three pendant lights are vintage. The two that look similar were made from old Pasadena streetlights.

COLOR CONSULTATION

SCHUYLER SAMPERTON DOES A QUICK MAKEOVER WITH
BENJAMIN MOORE SWISS COFFEE OC-45

"I did this in a guesthouse where the previous
owner had put in nasty fake terra-cotta tile. You
know that icky pale pink color? It drove me nuts!
I painted it white. It completely transformed
the space."

ANTHONY BARATTA FOSTERS A HOLIDAY MOOD WITH
BENJAMIN MOORE CARNIVAL RED 23

"I couldn't live without my red floors. Every floor
in my log cabin is red. It brings me this absolute
cheeriness. In summer, it feels like the Fourth of
July; in winter, it's like Christmas."

BRETT BELDOCK ENVELOPS THE WHOLE ROOM IN
BENJAMIN MOORE KITTEN WHISKERS 1003

"The reason I paint a floor is to get this sort of
tonal cocoon. I do the walls and the floor in the
same color so the eye goes around very softly. I like
this color because it's more than a beige. Sometimes it's strawberry yogurt and sometimes it's wet
sand, depending on the light."

A LOW-KEY KITCHEN GETS A SHOT OF POLISH WITH BLUE LACQUER FLOORS

"Blue—Benjamin Moore Deep Ocean 2058-30—was a natural for a Nantucket boathouse, and it brightened all that old wood. Then we spattered it with red, white, and blue, so you don't notice all the sand you track in. You just tap a wet paintbrush against a strip of wood, but it's more difficult to control than you think. It could end up looking like a Jackson Pollock—but that would be cool, too." —GARY McBOURNIE, DESIGNER

ONE POWERFUL FOCAL POINT MAKES A KITCHEN

A French limestone mantel is the focal point of this new kitchen. The 19th-century French chandelier was restored and wired.

"The fireplace isn't antique, we just knocked it with a mallet and chisel and rubbed some ashes on it. Almost everything in this room has been distressed— the stones on the floor, the beams in the ceiling, even the wood on the counter-tops." —LENTE-LOUISE LOUW SCHWARTZ, DESIGNER

"I found the cabinet at the Paris flea market and we designed the kitchen around it. This is an Edwardian brick house, built in 1905. The architect copied all the chunky moldings from the old house and had rippled restoration glass made for the cabinets. I supplied the vintage glass knobs, which I've been collecting for years." —SUSAN DOSSETTER, DESIGNER

The antique oak cabinet, originally made for a French store, is perfect for a collector. Susan Dossetter found the reproduction Windsor chairs on Nantucket and had the table made to work with the chairs and the cabinet. The floor is hand-rubbed wide-plank red oak.

DESIGNER
Master class

With an armload of hydrangeas for the kitchen table, which **VASE** would you use?

"This flower lends itself to mono-chromatic groupings. I'd do a mass of these mophead hydrangeas accented with blue lacecap hydrangeas to add some texture. The tall oval shape of the vase is perfect for this type of loose but simple arrangement."

—SEAN MCGOWAN,
FLORAL DESIGNER

VASE BY HENRY DEAN FROM
WILLIAMS-SONOMA HOME

"I love this cachepot because it hides the stems and you don't have to worry about keeping the water clean. For this container I would use lots of hydrangeas and group them into a very full mound, leaving just a few leaves around the top. This makes a perfect centerpiece for a casual dining table."

—BUNNY WILLIAMS, DESIGNER

TRELLIS WORK CACHEPOT FROM TREILLAGE

"Hydrangeas are easy to arrange. I'd use this ironstone pitcher to keep things simple. You should always leave the stems as long as possible so they touch the bottom of your vase and the flowers can absorb lots of water. And remember to keep your flowers out of the sun."

—MICHAEL GRIM, FLORAL DESIGNER

SYDENHAM SHAPE IRONSTONE PITCHER FROM BRIDGEHAMPTON FLORIST

"I like to use a bubble-shaped vase for hydrangeas and arrange them into a cloud. They should be asymmetrical and look imperfect. Always remove excess leaves to clean up the stems. Be sure to keep a little air between the blooms, too, so they can breathe."

—ROBERT RUFINO,
  STYLE EXPERT

BLUE ROSE BOWL FROM PLANTER RESOURCE

BEDROOMS

SOOTHING | SNUG | NATURAL

"There's something truly classic about bright white beadboard, but it can feel cliché. That's why we preserved all the cracks in the ceilings and the places where walls had bowed out over time. I think if we'd enclosed the walls and coated them with a perfect layer of plaster, the place would have lost something essential." —TOM STRINGER, DESIGNER

An antique circular mirror over a vintage-style Williams-Sonoma bed makes this guest room feel like it's filled with a cozy jumble of inherited pieces.

"Axel Vervoordt is a master at taking old objects and turning them into art. He'll cut the top off an old table and it will become an amazing fireplace screen. An example of that kind of repurposing is the way we used an old door as the master bedroom headboard."
—KAY DOUGLASS, DESIGNER

Ivy-pattern pillowcases are in Galbraith & Paul fabric and the pair of Earl chairs are from South of Market.

BEDROOMS

"First of all, it's about layering pattern on pattern. That's the secret. And don't go for matchy-matchy-matchy. I love these bright pinks and greens, and the juxtaposition of a William and Mary bed with that oversize photo looks so modern. It all marries incredibly well."
—KATHRYN IRELAND, DESIGNER

The bedspread and pillowcase with suns are from Ireland's own collection. The bolster pillow is made from an antique Suzani. Flower photo by Oberto Gili.

The lantern is an early California cowboy lamp.

"It's kind of a world of nations in this room. We've got a Suzani quilt, a kilim rug and pillows, a Shaker chair, and a Mexican wood chandelier. I haven't put bulbs in it yet. Every home should have at least one thing left undone."
—KELLY MCDOWELL, DESIGNER

AN ORNATE HEADBOARD FEELS
SOFT WHEN IT'S GENTLY AGED

"The headboard was part of a large cartouche that came from Austria. It's pine, and in two pieces mounted directly to the wall. We thought it was reminiscent of a chalet in Europe where you'd throw this one enormous piece in a room. It makes the room feel a little larger, and holds everything else together."
—MARSHALL WATSON, DESIGNER

....

The curls and swoops of the headboard are echoed in the curtains— Lee Jofa's Mayapore Crewel. A rustic twig mirror plays into the mix of casual and fantastical.

....

"In a small space like this you view things close at hand, so in many ways the detail is more important than it might be in a grander space."

INSPIRED OBSESSIONS
....
Basketry

Seagrass from Ralph Lauren Home

Field Baskets by Alice Ogden

Garden Baskets from Mitchell Gold + Bob Williams

Five Peck Field Basket from Texas Basket Company

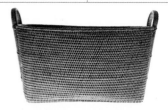

Nito Oversized Basket from Crate & Barrel

Rectangular Rush Basket from Beach Bungalow

Vine Basket from Bloom

"I have an obsession with anything that's woven. I love baskets, and I buy them all over the world—Morocco, Spain, France. If they can't fit in my luggage, then I'll wrap them around my luggage. It's just this great everyday item."
—VICTORIA PEARSON, DESIGNER AND PHOTOGRAPHER

BATHROOMS

"The leggy console instead of a cabinet makes our small bath feel larger."
—MELANIE POUNDS, DESIGNER

The marble sink was a flea-market find, and the black lacquer console was made to fit. Faucet by Newport Brass.

A Robinson Iron garden urn is reinvented as a powder room sink.

"The homeowners have done a lot of touring in England of various gardens, and I knew it was important to bring that love of gardens inside." —SUSAN FERRIER, DESIGNER

TRADITIONAL WITH A TWIST

Old-school silhouettes, patterns, and colors rooted in tradition, reinvented in fresh 21st-century ways

LEFT: **"When people walk in, they can't believe the house hasn't been here forever. But it's only fourteen years old. When we renovated, everything was done the way it would have been done in the 1920s or '30s, so it doesn't scream 'last year.'"** —FERN SANTINI, DESIGNER

OPPOSITE: **"The ceilings were critical. After they went up, the rooms instantly felt more intimate. We thought they needed to be the real deal—old wood. Our primary sources were antique long-leaf pine from old buildings that were being torn down. Their age gives them a great patina. They literally glow."** —FERN SANTINI, DESIGNER

ENTRYWAYS

"Tenting makes people feel so special. This foyer is womblike. Tenting is also quite practical because it muffles the street noise. And something happens when you put a gold-leaf console up against a humble ticking stripe wall, it becomes fresh and young. That's what I love." —**ALESSANDRA BRANCA, DESIGNER**

Tenting is in a Rogers & Goffigon ticking. Dennis & Leen Queen Anne side chairs flank an 18th-century Venetian gold-leaf console. Mirror from Atelier Branca Collection.

Glazed walls give the entry warmth, and the bold chevron carpet adds a casual touch. Settee is covered in Carleton V's Tamarack Stripe in Espresso. The antique Chinese lanterns and bamboo chairs are from James Sansum.

"I do love elegant old houses, and I'm not sure everyone knows how to make them comfortable. If I filled this place with mid-century furniture or 1970s chrome and glass like some people do today, it wouldn't work long-term. Eventually the rooms would feel like some time capsule of what's popular now. They'd wind up looking hilarious." —MARKHAM ROBERTS, DESIGNER

"The Chippendale mirror for the front entrance was being restored, and I'd only seen photos of it. Until I actually saw it, I didn't have the full sense of its scale. I had an initial panic attack about how it was going to work in the space. But, honestly, it knocks your socks off when you walk in—it's almost floor-to-ceiling."
—ASHLEY WHITTAKER, DESIGNER

The Chippendale mirror is meant for a huge room above a mantel or console, but the placement in a small foyer is a showstopper. Madagascar wallcovering and entry table from John Rosselli. Vaughan lantern.

Sanders framed favorite artworks with blue mats to make them stand out in the entry stairway.

"The way we hung the prints and drawings in that seemingly random way has the feeling of those wonderful English country houses. We took the biggest print, put it in the middle, and worked outward from there. Two items with the same theme couldn't be side by side unless they were part of a series. A horse couldn't be next to another horse. We couldn't put the same matting or frame next to each other." —SCOTT SANDERS, DESIGNER

LIVING ROOMS

"The concept was to feel like you were someplace else—a little fantasy. I used a custom-printed cotton in light moss green on the walls with black-green woodwork and touches of orange. The cocktail tables are new pieces based on a certain genre of exuberant, creative 18th-century Italian taborets, and I love their playfulness—the way they incorporate the past, but with a kick."
—ALESSANDRA BRANCA, DESIGNER

For old-world richness, Branca covered slipper chairs in Claremont's Brocatelle Le Griffon in Sulphur. Walls upholstered in Jaipur by Raoul Textiles. Lion-leg side tables from Dennis & Leen and gilt-bronze elephant sconces from Branca.

"The shapes are all rather traditional—the Billy Baldwin–inspired slipper chairs, the tufted ottoman by the fire, the Napoleon III chair covered in turquoise cashmere. It's the fabric that feels young. The bright green strié velvet on the sofa is unexpected and makes it less serious than it is. I wanted to have fun with the fabrics and color."
—ASHLEY WHITTAKER, DESIGNER

Slipper chairs are covered in Vizcaya in Celery by AM Collections. Faux-tortoise coffee table is from Todd Romano. Curtains are Granada in Robins Egg by AM Collections.

COLOR CONSULTATION

ALESSANDRA BRANCA IS DRAWN TO FINE PAINTS OF EUROPE E25

"The red I'm drawn to is softer than a lipstick red. It's been seasoned by time. Lacquer it on the walls with chalky trim for that lovely play of sheen and matte. In Renaissance portraits, there's always a shot of red. It adds punctuation and snap."

MARIO BUATTA CHANNELS NANCY LANCASTER WITH BENJAMIN MOORE LEMON MERINGUE 2023-50

"When I first saw Nancy Lancaster's famous 'buttah' yellow room back in the 1960s, I went berserk. I had to do my own rendition. Hers was more golden and mine was more pineapple, and then I hung lots of blue-and-white pottery and porcelain. People still ask me about that color."

BARCLAY BUTERA ECHOES AN ENGLISH MANOR WITH RALPH LAUREN PAINT MYSTIC RIVER SS21

"This reminds me of one of those great stately English home sort of blues, because it's got a touch of gray in it. The gray makes it feel more transparent."

**ELEGANCE ON LOAN, A WALL COLOR BORROWED FROM
9TH-CENTURY ENGLAND**
"The color is so warm and cozy that it makes you feel as if there's a fire in the
fireplace, even when there is none. It reminds me of those Regency period
interiors, with all those vivid colors inspired by the excavations at Pompeii.
We borrowed the unusual finish from the parlor of the Thomas Everard House
in Colonial Williamsburg where varnish is applied over your base paint."
—COURTNEY COLEMAN, DESIGNER

LIVING ROOMS

PATTERN ON PATTERN; A
TIME-HONORED WAY TO ADD WARMTH

"It's all a big mix, but basically
the vibration of each pattern
is sympathetic. They all have
that oxblood red in them.
With reds, I think they all go
together anyway. Red is a
kind of neutral to me."

"The house is a pretty 1940s Colonial—very *Bringing Up Baby*, and then we threw in a dash of *Auntie Mame*."
—MICHAEL S. SMITH, DESIGNER

....

"The desk behind one of the sofas acts as a visual anchor, and then the carpet has a very strong pattern that locks everything in place."

....

"The sofas are covered in a beautiful Braquenié fabric printed in France— Le Grand Genois, a classic 18th-century pattern that has been used by everybody from Sister Parish to Givenchy. What I love about it is that it's slightly off-kilter— there's so much white, which gives it a lightness. And it's not overly sweet—it has some spikes."

....

"Walls are a textured paper with a custom paint and glaze over it, which gives it more depth. That combination of red and yellow is just so appealing. Those colors have instant warmth."

STYLE SEMINAR
with Phoebe Howard

This Jacksonville–based designer says she keeps "two feet in the past and both eyes on the future." Follow her lead to create a Traditionalist living room of your own.

COVER THE SOFA IN SOFT TEXTURE
"I love small-scale matelassé fabrics, like Baker Fabric 41-629, on sofas. The quilted texture adds comfort."

UPHOLSTER CLUB CHAIRS IN A GOOD OLD-FASHIONED PRINT
"I was searching for a great old-fashioned print, but wanted something loose with sunny colors. I literally jumped when I found this—Garden Roses by Suzanne Rheinstein for Lee Jofa—it made me so happy."

SWATH A CHAISE IN SUMPTUOUS LINEN VELVET
"Cervo (in Alice) from Rogers & Goffigon is a scrumptious linen velvet, and a very pretty shade of blue."

WRAP SLIPPER CHAIRS IN A MOLTEN GOLD HUE
"The vermicelli embroidery on Wander from Lee Jofa adds dimension and a touch of whimsy."

AN OTTOMAN BY THE FIRE NEEDS COZY EMBROIDERY

"I call Kravet's Fabric 28779 the blender—
it's the one fabric that ties everything together.
Even though it's used in a small way, it's still
important."

UNLINED SILK CURTAINS AT THE WINDOWS
LITERALLY GLOW

"At certain times of the day, this silk (Chantel,
in pale gold from Nancy Corzine) at the windows
will bathe the room with a soft, warm glow.
Absolute sunshine."

FINISH IT OFF WITH CRISP STRIPE SOFA PILLOWS

"I like a crisp, tailored look for the pillows—
Lamorak through Zoffany keeps everything
from getting too feminine."

LIVING ROOMS

"In the living room there's a **Fortuny** silk chandelier that I hung over a cast-bronze ottoman. **N**ot everyone's aware of it, but the **V**enetian silk shape of that chandelier is based on the shape of an ancient **O**ttoman shield. And the ottoman beneath it, the one that centers the room, is also **T**urkish. It's made of cast bronze. I like to think of it as 'Edwardian on steroids.'"
—BARRY DIXON, DESIGNER

Rose Tarlow's gnarled twig table. Hakan Ezer ottoman.

Walls are bathed in a custom sand color and the red cotton curtains and red chenille sofa warm the neutral palette.

"I didn't want it to be super-traditional, or too modern, either. It is a compromise between the two, a classical feel, I think." —PAOLO MOSCHINO, DESIGNER

LIVING ROOMS

A TRADITIONAL BEACH HOUSE GETS A WASH OF WHITE

Espley-Miller's living room has an expansive view of the Pacific Ocean, a massive stone fireplace, and big, comfortable sofas and chairs slip-covered in white cotton denim. A "wonderfully huge" antique dhurrie defines the seating area. Walls are Benjamin Moore White Heron. The blue print throw is from Hermès.

"I'm not at all trendy—
I like to make houses
you can live in a
long time. I think of
white as a universal
color that you'll
never get tired of."
—CAROLYN ESPLEY-
  MILLER, DESIGNER

....

"Things can't be too
dainty when you use
this much white, or it'll
look way too sweet. I
had to ground it with
grays and browns and
blacks and big tex-
tured pieces. I wanted
light and white, but
not where everything
looked like it could
just up and float away."

....

"I'd never have done
white if they weren't
slipcovers. They
come off and on a lot.
But stains don't set
if someone fesses up
fast and we can get
it out quick."

....

"The blues were
inspired by those
Fortuny pillows on the
sofa. I saw them and
had an 'Aha!' moment.
What a fabulous color
for a beach house! It's
the blue of a Paraíba
tourmaline. So I
spread it around."

" **Book spines should line up with the front edge of each shelf, with no more than ¹/₈-inch of shelf showing. Arrange them according to height, but not in ascending order—make a gentle wave pattern so the eye goes up and down. Organize them so the colors look good. Mix in beautiful art and objects, placing them strategically in some faintly geometric pattern, maybe an X. One more thing: Banish your paperbacks to the basement!"**

—ELAINE GRIFFIN, DESIGNER

"Group books by subject or even color. Stand some upright, and then stack some horizontally to break the monotony. Mix in favorite pieces of pottery, collectibles, shells or family photos."

—ANGIE HRANOWSKY, DESIGNER

"People have wonderful art books but they rarely look at them. I bought a bookstand, set out one of my favorites, and now when I walk by I see a beautiful photograph. I turn the pages daily."

—PAUL VINCENT WISEMAN, DESIGNER

"If you have a dining table that stands dormant most of the time, turn it into a library table. Collect beautiful books and create small stacks around the perimeter of the table. Place a large-scale object—like a globe, a piece of sculpture, or a fantastic topiary—in the center. Then place a small object on top of each stack. I have used tea caddies, magnifying lenses, crystal spheres. Pick anything that interests you."

—THOMAS PHEASANT, DESIGNER

"I came up with shelves based on a design by the architect Hugh Newell Jacobsen. Each cubicle is a perfect square foot. We painted the room dark chocolate to highlight the geometry." —SIMON WATSON, DESIGNER

The library's high-gloss brown walls play up the grid pattern of the bookshelves. Pillows in Ixtapa by Jacques Bouvet et Cie make a handsome, well-worn chesterfield sofa look even more comfortable and inviting.

Tablescape

Furoshiki wrapping cloths through Aero Studios Ltd.

Pewter Stoneware from Juliska looks like antique pewter

Solid Luster glass egg place-card holder and silver porcelain miniature apple place-card holder from Aero Studios Ltd.

Reed & Barton's Marielle collection is based on a set of 18th-century Irish crystal

The embossed motif on O'Brien's stainless flatware from Reed & Barton was inspired by a Renaissance-era marble floor

"I like to combine modern and traditional, masculine and feminine, and colors—like the blue of my dinnerware against the rich wood tones of the table. A whimsical piece adds charm and surprise to a formal table. One of my favorites is this zinc rabbit." **—THOMAS O'BRIEN, DESIGNER**

Marielle Dinnerware, Marielle Indigo round bowl, Tiago slate-blue urn vase, Tiago candlesticks, all by Thomas O'Brien for Reed & Barton, zinc rabbit available at Aero Studios Ltd.

DINING ROOMS

"People always ask, 'What kind of wallpaper is that?' It's actually hand-painted. The idea was to do a chinoiserie white scene—white trees, white leaves, all very whitewashed, a little like a fresco." —PAOLO MOSCHINO, DESIGNER

The dining room feels European. The ceiling is dominated by a 19th-century French bronze and crystal chandelier.

"I wanted the dining room to be a beautiful winter garden in the middle of downtown Chicago."

"In 18th-century France they did the fancy fabric on the front of the chairs and a simple plaid or check on the back. These chairs are in the style of Louis XVI, but they're a play on that era's classic tradition, a wonderful twist. Linen velvet on the fronts, taffeta stripes on the backs. I do this a lot."
—ALESSANDRA BRANCA, DESIGNER

DINING ROOMS

Queen Anne–style chairs are covered in Braquenié's Coromandel and backed with a Brunschwig & Fils velvet, Botticelli in Olive. Roberts designed the blown-up Chinese medallion rug and the red linen-covered console. The pair of lamps, from James Sansum, are made from 19th-century Chinese vases. Tole chandelier by Vaughan.

"Vibrant, shining green takes the fuddy-duddy out of this formal room."
—MARKHAM ROBERTS, DESIGNER

....

"Just because there's a big Georgian table in a big formal dining room doesn't mean there's a butler serving dinner. This room is octagonal and serious, but the walls are all wild and bright."

....

"I specifically said to myself, 'You are not going to use an old Georgian sideboard or Chippendale chairs here.' The owners give long, long dinner parties where guests sit forever talking and laughing. You can't sit forever in a Chippendale chair. You can sink into these chairs and enjoy yourself all night."

STYLE SEMINAR
with Barry Dixon

This Virginia designer bridges past and present with heart-stopping results. His favorites showcase Traditional with a Twist at its best.

1

2

6

1. **Stationery:** William Arthur through Copenhaver, Washington, D.C.

2. **Lamp:** Donghia's Gigante Venetian glass floor lamp, any color

3. **Bed Pillow:** Yves Delorme's all-down pillow

4. **Car Color (exterior/interior):** Metallic silver/green

5. **Coffee or Tea:** Green jasmine tea or, on the run, Starbucks's venti sugar-free hazelnut latte

6. **Everyday Dishes:** Antique brown-and-white transferware

7. **Lightbulb/Wattage:** Satco's 7W frosted candle tip. Same wattage as a burning candle—perfect for those 18-arm chandeliers. No shades required.

8. **Showerhead:** Waterworks Etoile series 8" rose

9. **Mattress:** Serta Perfect Sleeper with down pad

10. **Picture Frame:** Bottega Veneta's woven leather

11. **Scented Candle or Room Fragrance:** Jo Malone Orange Blossom

12. **All-purpose Glass:** Williams-Sonoma's Sienna glass with Nito natural woven vine sleeve

13. **Sofa Shape:** Knole sofa with bolster pillows

14. **Towel:** Waterworks

15. **Chair:** Barrymore from my line with Tomlinson/Erwin-Lambeth

16. **Wallpaper:** Adelphi wallpapers—historic and eco-friendly

17. **Workhorse Fabric:** Cotton or linen velvet. I'm loving Vervain's Venue series right now.

Niermann Weeks
Avignon chandelier;
Swaim dining chairs in
Bergamo's Siegfried
fabric; Barcelona table
by Panache Designs

"I used all the abstractions of nature—earth, air, fire, water, and heavenly bodies.
It puts a house in a place beyond fads. The dark bare floor suggests earth.
The wave shape at the bottom of the roman shade brings in a water element.
The base of the antique Portuguese table has a hand-carved vine on it. Then
the curtain's fabric is fire—common hemp with gilt fibers woven through it."
—BARRY DIXON, DESIGNER

DINING ROOMS

"I love those wing chairs. I put a coarse linen print on them in a large-scale pattern because they seemed to me to need a really strong fabric. Then I added the small horn handles to the backs so the men could pull them away from the table." —NANCY BOSZHARDT, DESIGNER

The antique mahogany dining table, which opens to seat twelve, is encircled by wing chairs, designed by Boszhardt, with unusually decorative spiral legs. The chairs are covered in a Rose Tarlow linen, Medici in Sienna on Wheat. Chandelier is from Bermingham & Co.

"We found these beautiful Swedish whitewashed armchairs, but only three. So we made up the difference with three more tall classic dining chairs. One set's in a botanical print, the other in leather. Our goal was to do a dining room that is elegant, but also friendly." —**SUZANNE KASLER, DESIGNER**

Kasler alternated two different chairs with different coverings—Edelman leather and a Clarence House print. The same print, **Arts and Crafts in green**, was used for the curtains. **Custom walnut table, Ainsworth-Noah.**

KITCHENS
....

"The backsplash is old reclaimed tile from France that was probably on the floor of some château. It was kind of a gutsy direction for me, to do such a bold backsplash. But when I saw that tile—the colors, the simplicity, the realness of it—I knew I had to have it for this kitchen." —**SHANNON BOWERS**, DESIGNER

French concrete tiles were purchased at **Chateau Domingue** in Houston. Concrete countertops were cast in place and finished with an acrylic sealer and a special wax. To maintain the patina, they're re-waxed about every two months.

"In movies like *Gosford Park*, I'm always looking at all the back-of-the-house stuff. I wanted to play up the idea that this was a great old service kitchen. Edwin Lutyens, the great English architect, was all about shape, and this is my Lutyens barrel-vault ceiling. It gives a sense of ceremony to a narrow space."
—MICHAEL S. SMITH, DESIGNER

The hanging lights under the barrel vault are from Ann-Morris Antiques. The refrigerator is by Sub-Zero. The floor is reclaimed fumed brown oak.

KITKENS

THE EAT-IN KITCHEN, REINVENTED, WHERE AN ANTIQUE TABLE DOUBLES AS THE ISLAND

Louis XV–style dining chairs—played down in Donghia's Relaxed Linen in Storm—mix with a 19th-century French farm table and silver-leaf Capucine chandelier from Niermann Weeks. The Roman shade is in Galbraith & Paul's Zinnia in Sky.

"We didn't want to do one of those typical island kitchens, so we put an ancient French farm table right in the middle of the room in front of the butler's sink."
—SUZANNE KASLER, DESIGNER

"The roman shade is in a print of stylized zinnias from Galbraith & Paul, very fun and fresh."

"The chairs are antiques with painted frames that we left just as we found them, but the linen dresses them down."

Island Hangovers

Savoy Pendant Light from Urban Archaeology

Glass Pineapple Lantern from Charles Edwards

Clemson Pendant from Restoration Hardware

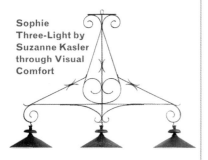

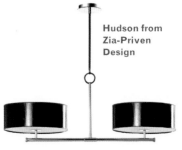

Sophie Three-Light by Suzanne Kasler through Visual Comfort

Hudson from Zia-Priven Design

"The lights over the island are 18th-century Portuguese lanterns, and they were a spectacular find! The fact that we were able to find a set of four is astounding. They still have bits of old candle wax on the inside, and they even have the original red paint on the polychrome." **—FERN SANTINI, DESIGNER**

Cabinets are in Benjamin Moore Nantucket Gray and are treated with a custom sienna glaze. Backsplash tiles are Torquemada Diamonds by Ann Sacks. Sanford stools by Minton-Spidell.

KITKCHENS

THE NEW NON-KITCHENS: BEAUTIFUL
SPACES THAT HAPPEN TO HAVE STOVES

"For a long time, the trend has been to make the kitchen as big and important
as possible. This is a beautiful space that happens to function as a kitchen for a
family with three young kids. The adjacent pantry is the backstage component.
That's where you'll find the clean-up sink, the dishes, the dry storage."
—KEN PURSLEY, ARCHITECT

Storage is hidden behind touch-latch doors in the paneling. Sofa designed
by Craig Dixon of Pursley Architecture. Stool by Teena Ironworks. Rug from
Brocade Home.

The kitchen doubles as an informal dining area and wine-tasting room. Fork and spoon prints from Branca. Lights from Urban Archaeology. Calacatta marble island.

"In the kitchen we wanted to carry a brown tone over from the dining room, but we also wanted black cabinets, so we wove them together with a brown-and-black-striped floor." —ALESSANDRA BRANCA, DESIGNER

COLOR CONSULTATION

BOLD WALLS INVIGORATE TRADITIONAL HALLWAY MOLDINGS:
DESIGNERS CHOOSE SOME OF THEIR FAVORITE HUES

TOM STRINGER CREATES DARK INTEREST WITH BENJAMIN
MOORE VAN BUREN BROWN HC-70

"I always think it's a mistake to try to make an interior room look brighter with white. I'd rather make it dark and interesting. I just used this color in a great Georgian house with beautiful white moldings and pedimented doorways in an eggshell finish, so you get a bit of sheen."

ELIZABETH BAUER GETS ROMANTIC WITH FARROW & BALL
BLACK BLUE 95

"I like black in a small hallway. Clients think you're crazy at first, but it's very romantic. This is not lifeless, like some blacks. The blue in it makes it warmer. It would be even better with a black and white marble floor."

SUE BURGESS LIKES OFF-WHITE TRIM WITH BENJAMIN
MOORE TAUPE 2110-10

"This is more molasses than chocolate, a wonderful color that's neutral and exciting at the same time. If you have traditional moldings, do them in off-white to set up a dramatic contrast. People are often afraid of dark colors. Try it. You'll like it."

ARCHES FEEL IMPORTANT AND REGAL WHEN ACCENTUATED BY BOLD COLOR

"Why do people treat hallways as a lonely, pathetic passageway? I love to see seating, even if nobody's actually going to sit. Add arched doorways so the space seems less rectilinear. Give it a waist with wainscoting. I did the walls in a delicious burnt orange—Farrow & Ball Orangery 70, the color of candied orange peel." —DARREN HENAULT, DESIGNER

Wall Flowers

Arabella in Celadon from Designers Guild through Osborne & Little

Magnolia by David Easton for Cole & Son

Magnolia Sidewall from Sandpiper Studios

China Rose in Boudoir from Carleton V

Reddish Rose in Black on White by Albert Hadley through Hinson & Co.

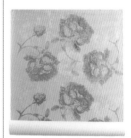

Rose du Roi in Chartreuse from TylerGraphic

"I wanted to do a pretty, fancy lady's dressing room for my client as part of the master suite. I said, 'This is your space, only for you, let's just do it in this wonderful old-fashioned chintz.'" **—MARKHAM ROBERTS, DESIGNER**

Chintz-covered walls in Hydrangea & Rose in Green and Pink by Travers.

BEDROOMS

"This ceiling is so powerful, I had to scale everything back and keep it simple. We tried a painting over the bed, but it felt like an intruder."
—ELEANOR CUMMINGS, DESIGNER

Wood beams and antique Parefeuille tile are juxtaposed on the ceiling. The walls are plaster. Bedding by Leontine Linens.

"She loves the floral on the walls, the celestial blues, the cloudlike feeling. He loves the neutrals, and the way the room envelops and soothes him."
—KIRSTEN FITZGIBBONS, DESIGNER

The Manuel Canovas wallcovering is a strong pattern, but the soft colors make it a livable choice for a bedroom. Platinum leafing on the bed frame brings in a little shimmer.

"I look at that armoire as the largest medicine cabinet in the world. Armoires are good solutions in a room without enough storage. They don't cannibalize as much space as a closet, and they're a nice decorative element. And we upholstered the chairs with terry cloth over an outdoor fabric."
—BARRY DIXON, DESIGNER

A custom lattice armoire with sandblasted glass doors by Oly provides storage for linens and toiletries. Walker Zanger tiles.

"I don't think your most precious pieces have to go in the living room. My client spends a lot of time in her bath, and this way she can look at things like the 19th-century English secretary every day."
—PAOLO MOSCHINO, DESIGNER

MODERNIST

Clean lines, tailored detail,
and luminous color deployed
with an eye for the utmost
balance and serenity

LEFT: "**We wanted a paneled library, but not traditional wood paneling. It's also not a very big room, so we did it in white squares, which is a more modern idea of paneling. To make it more interesting, the dark line is an inset of bronze.**" —**DAVID KLEINBERG, DESIGNER**

OPPOSITE: "**The fact of the matter is, everything doesn't go together. I'm sorry, but it just doesn't. I've always adhered to the same principles—proportion, suitability, comfort.**" —**DAVID KLEINBERG**

ENTRYWAYS

NO TCHOTCHKES | NO FRILLS | LOTS AND LOTS OF DRAMA

"It's about clean and simple. I wanted everything to have a chunky, useful, casual quality to it, and a similar level of detail. I didn't want pieces with too much intricacy." —STEVEN GAMBREL, DESIGNER

Gambrel wanted the foyer to communicate that "dogs, kids, and bare feet" are welcome. The sculptural spotlight by the stairs is a vintage English ship light from R.E. Steele.

"When you're working on a small scale house like this, simple is always better. So we painted the walls a clean white and gave the original floors, which were wide pine boards, a coat of cool gray . . ."
—ALBERT HADLEY, DESIGNER

On the table that marks an imaginary "center hall" in the house, Asian wood figures surround a bronze censer. A well-polished oil barrel holds the owner's collection of new and old canes.

Leading Lights

**Bretton from
Seagull Lighting**

**Brighton Hall Lantern
from the Bill Sofield
Collection through Baker**

**Wisteria Hanging
Lamp D from Eric
Brand Furniture**

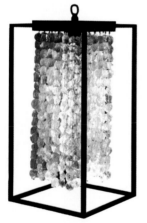

**Alex Pendant from Fuse
Lighting by Kevin Kolanowski**

**Heron Lantern from
Remains Lighting**

**Gothic Three-
Light Lantern by
Visual Comfort**

"People like airy spaces. The way the Scandinavians bring
light into a room." **—ALEXANDRA ANGLE, DESIGNER**

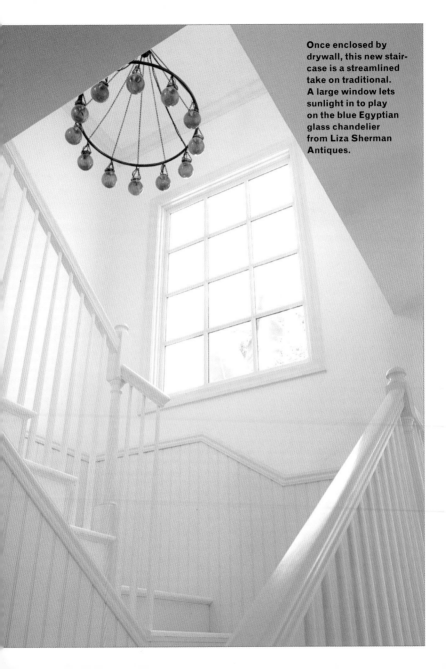

Once enclosed by drywall, this new staircase is a streamlined take on traditional. A large window lets sunlight in to play on the blue Egyptian glass chandelier from **Liza Sherman Antiques.**

LIVING ROOMS

....

PEACEFUL | SOOTHING | BALANCED

"Pristine white, clean lines, symmetry, neatness: that's what I call serenity. I always strive to make everything perfect—exactly 15 inches of knee space between the coffee table and the sofa, that kind of thing."
—**LINDSEY BOND, DESIGNER**

Bond removed moldings and the mantel to clean up the architecture. Wall-mounted shelves eliminate the need for more furniture.

The living room is divided into two seating areas. A pair of Tiplady Knole sofas from George Smith face each other in front of the fireplace. The same Todd Hase silk, Rice, is on all the upholstered pieces.

"We tried to infuse it with a feeling of light and warmth. The whole interior is made of this pale gold wood, with pale limestone fireplaces. The floors on the main level are all pale bleached oak, with pale gold sisal in the living room."
—GREG STEWART, DESIGNER

LIVING ROOMS

EVEN A FARMHOUSE IS SEXY
WHEN INTERIORS ARE STREAMLINED

A wall of glass-paned doors folds open, creating a seamless flow from indoors to outdoors. Ebanista's Vienna Angled sofa floats between the living and dining areas. Folding doors are by NanaWall.

"It's easy to be flashy. It's far more difficult to be subtle and still get your point across."
—JEAN LARETTE, DESIGNER

"There are farmhouse elements like the planked ceiling. But I also wanted the house to be sophisticated and elegant and sexy."

"It's all about restraint, restraint, restraint. There's not a lot of stuff around, not even a lot of table lamps. Restraint is elegant; it's the key to serenity."

"I like solids—I'd rather create visual interest with texture than with pattern. If I do use pattern—on a throw pillow, say—it isn't a dainty pattern, it's a big geometric design. Even in rugs I like repeating geometric patterns."

"I don't respond to florals at all. I just think they look too grandmotherly and I don't use too many colors in one room."

COLOR CONSULTATION

STEVEN GAMBREL COMES BACK AGAIN AND AGAIN TO
BENJAMIN MOORE HORIZON 1478

"I always come back to Horizon, a pale gray that
doesn't turn blue or green on you. It's a sophisticated, perfect background to so many interiors.
Blues, of course, look beautiful against this gray,
but so do pinks, lavenders, and the legs of sofas and
chairs that have been stained a driftwood color."

ELLEN KENNON WILL PAINT A WHOLE HOUSE FULL
SPECTRUM PAINTS MUSHROOM

"I'll do entire houses in Mushroom, which is
pretty darned fabulous. It's a beige, but it changes
drastically—one minute it's putty and the next,
it's rosier. Chameleon-like and mysterious, it takes
on the properties of the colors around it."

JENNIFER GARRIGUES QUIETS THE MOOD WITH BENJAMIN
MOORE MESQUITE 501

"Mesquite is a flattering light moss green without
much yellow. I love it because it doesn't shout 'I'm
green!' It says, 'I'm a very beautiful color.'"

A SMOKY LAVENDER NEUTRAL HAS BOTH REFINEMENT AND SEX APPEAL

"I've been using **C2 Bella D**onna a lot. It's a smoky lavender gray, the color of a twilight sky. I used it on the parlor floor of a brownstone and it looked flat-out sophisticated. Bella Donna is a sexy, adult color, but it can go a lot of different ways." —**DD ALLEN, DESIGNER**

LIVING ROOMS

"I think my rooms are sensual because of the balance of shapes and the blending of colors in different shadings, depths and textures."
—**VICENTE WOLF**, DESIGNER

An antique painted birch chair from **Sweden** is upholstered in **Classic Cloth's Faille Tafffeta**. The gridded mirror propped against the wall is a **Vicente Wolf** design. Sofa is covered in **Cowtan & Tout's Bonsai boucle in Clay**. The yellow throw pillows are in a **Cowtan & Tout** ribbed cotton.

The 22-foot-high ceilings are grounded by a set of 1940s oak frame chairs, two coffee tables from France, and a Jean-Michel Frank–style sofa.

"I had a clear vision and I always knew I wanted a sky blue palette. The furniture plan is very symmetrical—a sofa flanked by four chairs, basically. There's a fire-place at one end and behind the kitchen there's a little bedroom. I think I could live there so happily. It's all I would need." —DAVID KLEINBERG, DESIGNER

LIVING ROOMS

MID-CENTURY CLASSICS
KEEP THE MOOD SERENE

Craftsman was the modern of its time, and it goes surprisingly well with modernist furniture like the Le Corbusier **LC 5** daybed. Hom mixed mid-century classics with contemporary pieces, and painted all the walls white to make his **California Craftsman** bungalow feel current. A **Piero Lissoni Jelly** table holds a sculpture from the **Alameda flea market**, one of Hom's favorite places to shop.

"I don't want my house to look overly analyzed, but it's very studied. To me, a big part of the beauty of an object is what it's next to."
—AARON HOM, DESIGNER AND STYLIST

....

"The white candlestick on the mantel goes away against the white wall, but then the way it cuts in front of the frame of the painting, just a little bit, is so pretty. And the way the shape of the painting mimics the shape of the fireplace below creates a symmetry that's pleasing."

....

"I used lots of different Benjamin Moore whites here. To me, a room with just one shade of white feels antiseptic—blah, not much depth. The woodwork is painted Pure White, and the walls are Snow White. I painted the living room brick in the fireplace Ice Mist in satin for a bit more contrast."

This Washington D.C. designer is inspired by the order and symmetry of classical architecture. His collection of furniture for Baker provides the building blocks of a Modernist living room.

ADD A SPARK OF REFLECTIVE IMPACT

"The Icon is very three-dimensional, more a wall appliqué. Instead of a mirror, that's a Lucite lens in the center. It's inspired by a piece in my Paris apartment. I think it would look great in any place you want impact but not a reflection. And wouldn't it look nice floating on top of a large mirror?"

FIND A PLACE FOR A SURPRISING GLASS CHANDELIER

"The glass in the Facet Chandelier lights up just like the base of the table lamp. The crystal and gold finial captures the light and sends a bit of shine into the room."

CAP IT OFF WITH A GROUP OF SCULPTURAL CHAIRS

"I love the shape of the Bel-Air Lounge Chair so much. It's so lean and sculptural. Group four in a living room. It has real presence."

SLIDE A BENCH UNDER A CONSOLE

"I like the modest scale of this bench. I used leather on the sides and base, chenille for the seat—I like to mix textures in similar colors. The nailheads create the boundary between the different fabrics."

ADD A TABLE LAMP WITH SUBTLE BRILLIANCE

"With the Facet Table Lamp we started with the shape. I wanted a faceted cone but wasn't sure about the material. I thought maybe rock crystal or glass. So we went to Italy and made one with glass and illuminated it. That's when we saw how elegantly the shaft lights up. It was really spectacular!"

CHOOSE AN ARMCHAIR THAT'S POWERFUL IN ITS SIMPLICITY

"My St. Germain armchair is a classic upholstered chair that would fit in any room, modern or traditional. In my own home I have a traditional table surrounded by ivory leather chairs. It's a mix I like."

DESIGNER
Master class

" **I like a classic shape: It will fit anywhere. And I don't skimp. A sofa with a well-made frame and eight-way hand-tied springs in the seat deck can last 30 years. Re-covering usually costs less than half the price of a new sofa.**"
—GARY HUTTON

"I think the back should be 50/50 or 75/25 down-and-feather fill, but the seat shouldn't be that soft. A foam core wrapped in down or a down-and-feather combination gives you a little more support for your bottom."
—ERIKA BRUNSON

"A sofa should look good from the back, in case you want to liberate it from the wall and float it in a room somewhere down the line."
—MALCOLM JAMES KUTNER

"I stay away from over-scaled sofas with those big, sweeping, curved arms. They take up valuable space and look like a set piece from *Dynasty*."
—JOE LUCAS

"Seat height is the most over-looked comfort measurement when people buy a sofa. I don't want it to be so low that your knees fly up when you sit down, or so high that your feet barely touch the floor. I like a seat height of 18 to 19 inches."
—WHITNEY STEWART

"I never recommend anything under 86 inches long. But I don't go over 100 inches. There are very few rooms that can handle a piece of furniture at that scale."
—LARRY LASLO

The custom sofa is upholstered in Lime linen from VW Home, with throw pillows covered in Frost from Norbar Fabrics in White and Parchment. Eero Saarinen's Womb chairs from Knoll face the lime-rubbed oak coffee table inset with a circle of concrete. The rug is made from squares of calfskin saddle-stitched together.

"A high-backed sofa envelops you like a cocoon and creates a sense of warmth and intimacy in a large living room. You could lie down for a nap and nobody would know you were there." —VICENTE WOLF

INSPIRED OBSESSIONS

Tablescape

Napoli Vintage Napkins from Libeco Home

Vera Naturals Tall Glass from Wedgwood

Oval Wine Cooler from Aero Studios Ltd.

Lemon Wood Bowl through Ochre

Wine Label Carafes from the Country Collection by William Yeoward.

Silver Aster Fine Bone China from Wedgwood

"Do what reflects you. For me, it's mixing my china collections. Target, Ikea, the 18th century . . . I love good design, I don't care where it's from. And I'm not a place mat kind of person. Probably because I like to have more room for china on the table." **—TRICIA FOLEY, DESIGNER AND AUTHOR**

Bowls, Wedgwood Vera Wang; white glasses, Ikea; napkins, Nicole Farhi; teapot, silver ice bucket, and salt dish, Foley's own.

DINING ROOMS

"When we first started talking about the floating sideboard I suggested goat-skin or shagreen. The husband happened to be holding a fountain pen with a knurled barrel, and he just dropped it on the table, saying, 'How about some-thing like that?' I extrapolated on the texture of the pen, and designed the console drawers in metal mesh." —FRANKLIN SALASKY, DESIGNER

The aluminum-and-glass Schlitz Up hanging light in the dining room is by Ingo Maurer. Cab leather dining chairs from Moss. Wall-mounted console by B Five Studio. Stained a dark walnut, the basket-weave floor is original to the pre-war apartment.

Wolf created a flexible loftlike living area. The L-shaped banquette and the ottoman are covered in wipeable polyester, Incognito Pearl in Glacier, from Designtex. Wolf designed the oval cast-concrete and chrome table. The inlaid chairs are from India. Walls are painted Benjamin Moore Super White.

"See those inlaid Indian chairs? You might think I was crazy to put them into such a minimal room, but I like that they look like they just landed there. The more subtle I can make a room, the more me-as-decorator fades into the background." —VICENTE WOLF, DESIGNER

DINING ROOMS

A SAARINEN DINING TABLE GOES WITH
EVERYDAY. IT'S A SIMPLE ELEGANT CHOICE

The large **George Nelson
Bubble Lamp** does a great job
of attracting attention. **Knoll's
Saarinen** marble table and
Tulip chairs are "pleasingly
thrown off" by the worn
vintage chair in the corner.

"The dining room
is all about the
ceiling. I thought
it was important
to play off that.
I love that round
lamp within the
box-beam grid
on the ceiling
. . . that's just
thrilling to me."
—**AARON HOM,
DESIGNER**

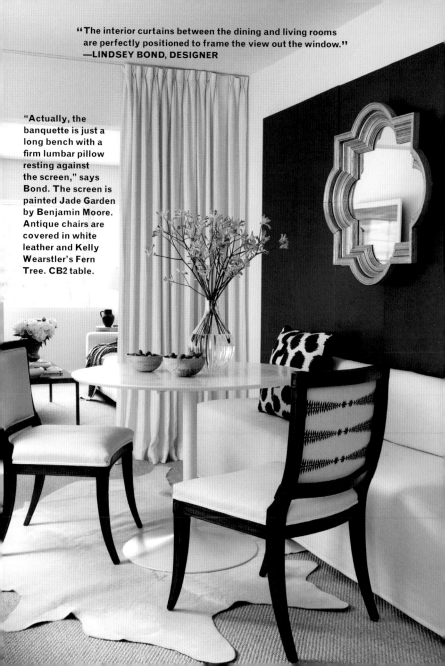

"The interior curtains between the dining and living rooms are perfectly positioned to frame the view out the window." —LINDSEY BOND, DESIGNER

"Actually, the banquette is just a long bench with a firm lumbar pillow resting against the screen," says Bond. The screen is painted Jade Garden by Benjamin Moore. Antique chairs are covered in white leather and Kelly Wearstler's Fern Tree. CB2 table.

STYLE SEMINAR
with Steven Gambrel

This New York City designer uses broad swathes of color in his uncommonly lovely projects. His favorite things illustrate a very special Modernist point of view.

6

14

1. **Everyday Dishes:** Crate & Barrel Marin White Dinnerware

2. **Artist:** Cy Twombly

3. **Bed Pillow:** Medium support by Laura Ashley

4. **Car Color (exterior/interior):** Chocolate brown

5. **Cleaning Supply:** Mrs. Meyer's Lemon Verbena

6. **Color:** Iceberg, Benjamin Moore #2122-50

7. **All-purpose Glasses:** CB2 Marta glasses

8. **Kitchen Gadget:** Standard meat thermometer

9. **Lamp:** Vintage pottery lamps

10. **Lightbulb/Wattage:** Reproduction Filament Edison bulb, 40W, from Just Bulbs, NYC

11. **Mattress:** From Long's Bedding—manufacturer: Aireloom. Style: Vitagenic. Firm mattress 9" thick, cotton ticking. All natural, cotton batting inside

12. **Sheets:** Casa del Bianco on Lexington Ave., NYC

13. **Soap:** L'Occitane lavender with wheat exfoliant—green bar with oatmeal in the bar

14. **Scented Candle or Room Fragrance:** Patchouli by Diptyque

15. **Workhorse Fabric:** Mokum Textiles #7111 Fez, especially in Quartz

"They're all armchairs. And it's a round table, so it's very democratic—there's no head." —STEVEN GAMBREL, DESIGNER

A 1950s Italian light fixture mixes easily with a black walnut Bron table from **BDDW** and eight vintage Alexandria chairs by Edward Wormley. The seat fabric is **Wet Martini** from Keleen Leathers. The rug is Linen Chevron in Camel from **ABC Carpet & Home.**

DINING ROOMS

THE WARMTH OF WOOD SOFTENS THE MACHINED
LINES OF MODERN TABLES AND CHAIRS

Chandelier with onyx shades is from Ironies. The wall color, Benjamin Moore Coventry Gray, was pulled from the Raimonds Staprans painting. Larette designed the rug, based on an iron grate she saw in Paris. Siren dining chairs by Holly Hunt.

"I love chocolate brown. My little black dress is always brown! And that gorgeous rustic teak dining table looks fantastic with all the blue."
—JEAN LARETTE, DESIGNER

"I wanted the furniture to relate more to driftwood than to a redwood, more ocean than inland. The chairs have caning, which, to me, says breezy and beachy, like the openness of the dining table base. I wanted the large furniture to be very see-through."
—CHRIS BARRETT, DESIGNER

Barrett designed the 1950s-style table and chairs. Chair fabric is **Classic Cloth's Gladestone.**

DESIGNER
Master class

What would you pair with a **PARSONS DESK WITH DRAWERS** from West Elm?

"This chair is a 1930s design, and its modernist lines go well with the desk's simplicity: the Parsons table was also designed in the '30s, by a student of Jean-Michel Frank."

—PETER DUNHAM

CLOUD CLUB CHAIR IN FAUBOURG LEATHER THROUGH HOLLYWOOD AT HOME.

"I've always loved the elegance of Hans Wegner's iconic 1955 swivel chair and its mix of wood, leather, and chrome. The more organic forms of the chair soften the geometry of the desk. Separately, the pieces have a simple beauty. Together, they make a rather bold statement, even if the understated spirit remains."

—BRAD FORD

SWIVEL CHAIR BY HANS WEGNER THROUGH DANISH DESIGN STORE.

"The Parsons desk is a blank canvas kind of piece. It's basic, and nicely proportioned—the best things come down to good proportions. The chair is more decorative. I'd describe this duo as perfectly balanced."

—LAURA KIRAR

CHARLA SIDE CHAIR BY LAURA KIRAR THROUGH BAKER.

"You can give this desk any personality, go any way with it. For me, a mix of unexpected elements is what creates great style. The desk is clean and tailored while the chair is slipcovered. I like the look of to-the-floor linen with the desk's hard edges."

—SUZANNE KASLER

HIGH BACK VILLA CHAIR BY JOHN SALADINO.

KITCHENS

DELICIOUS | CLEAN | ZESTY

"We took an ordinary storage shelf and turned it on the diagonal, so it looks more like an art piece. You can still see through it, but it sets off this more intimate area—a spillover space, a place to relax on a comfortable sofa."
—JEFF LEWIS, DESIGNER and star of Bravo's *Flipping Out*

KraftMaid's Brockton cabinetry. CaesarStone island and countertops. Brushed-aluminum counter stools from Design Within Reach. Kariota backsplash tiles from Walker Zanger. Zanzibar Antique Elm flooring by Mohawk.

The island is topped with a thick slab of Calacatta Gold marble. The back counter, in contrast, is topped with Pietra Cardosa, a dark, slatelike stone. White tile on backsplash by Waterworks. Barstools from Mig and Tig.

"A dark wood floor makes the line where it meets the white walls very crisp, and that makes the whole room feel cool and clean. Yet, at the same time, the dark wood is warm. It's nice to have some counterpoint. There's something so serene about white, but you don't want it to get boring."
—MICK DE GIULIO, KITCHEN DESIGNER

KITCHENS

OPEN SHELVING AND BRIGHT PATTERNED
SHADES LIGHTEN THE LOOK OF A BROWN KITCHEN

**Classic Norman Cherner plywood chairs
surround a vintage stone-topped table.
For casual dining at the Gascogne Blue
limestone island, barstools from a restaurant
supply store are in blue leather. Pendant
lights from Urban Archaeology; flush-mount
lights from Remains; 1940s rope chandelier.**

"We've all seen gorgeous white kitchens, and there's a place for them. I was trying to create something modern and clean. But I thought bringing in the colors of nature—silvers, grays, oysters, driftwoods, and sands—would be more appropriate."
—STEVEN GAMBREL, DESIGNER

....

"When there's no recessed lighting, you really need all of these light fixtures. The flush-mounted ones have a utilitarian look and furnish good general lighting. The pendants over the island and sink add additional task lighting. The rope chandelier is more decorative and helps define the dining area as a separate space. I also think they all look really good together."

KITCHENS

"I thought it would be fun to have a funky stainless steel fireplace surround. But I also wanted a delineation. An interesting ceiling can accomplish that. So I decided to vault the ceiling in the dining area. It's 14 feet high and when you look up, it's like it's open to the sky." —MICHALENE BUSICO, DESIGNER

A gas fireplace with a stainless steel surround is raised to eye level. Louis Ghost chairs from Design Within Reach surround a Calligaris wenge wood and glass dining table. The commercial-grade rug is by Masland.

"I thought since we're spending so much time here, let's be able to build a fire and really enjoy it. We elevated the fireplace so you can see the fire from wherever you are in the room. And I put the wood right underneath, because if you have to go outside to get it you're less likely to do it."
—WILLIAM HEFNER, ARCHITECT

Calacatta gold marble balances all the wood. The marble slab on the island looks even thicker with a 2¹/4-inch edge detail. Wall paint is Pratt & Lambert Chalk Gray.

BEDROOMS

MEDITATIVE | CALMING | AIRY

"I think for a married couple, their room should be slightly on the feminine side. A woman feels more comfortable in these colors and this increases a feeling of romance. Nothing is really pink-pink here, but all the fabrics have some aspect of blush to them." —SALLY MARKHAM, DESIGNER

A Ralph Lauren mink throw is draped over the imposing silk-upholstered bed designed by Markham.

"The headboard is lightly quilted linen, and it runs the entire length of one short wall in the master bedroom. It incorporates the bedside tables and reading lights, so it took a cabinetmaker and an electrician to pull it together."
—FRANKLIN SALASKY, DESIGNER

The headboard, in quilted Rogers & Goffigon linen, was designed by Salasky to include Estiluz wall lights from Lee's Studio and floating storage units.

COLOR CONSULTATION

MODERNISTS ALWAYS SELECT THE CALMEST COLORS FOR BEDROOM WALLS. DESIGNERS CHOOSE SOME OF THEIR FAVORITE HUES.

JENNIFER GARRIGUES BRINGS ON COZINESS WITH BENJAMIN MOORE SEASHELL OC-120

"This reminds me of the lightest color inside a shell—a little warmer than white. It makes me think of days in India after a cup of tea on the terrace and then a nap. It would turn a bedroom into a lovely retreat."

MICHAEL SIMON EVOKES PEACE WITH SHERWIN-WILLIAMS TOPSAIL SW6217

"I can't say it's aqua and I can't say it's gray. It's in the space between those colors. It's a very pale blue, and blue is a color that evokes calm. When the clouds clear and the sky displays its depths, or water reflects and distorts the sky, it reveals shades that defy description. Blue transports you."

ELISSA CULLMAN SOOTHES WITH BENJAMIN MOORE CELERY SALT 938

"This is a lovely pale green, dreamy and soothing, that worked really well for a young couple's master bedroom. And I love the name of the color—celery salt is the secret ingredient in my Bloody Marys!"

"I was looking for something different and chose this charcoal gray—
Benjamin Moore Kendell Charcoal. The high contrast between the dark walls
and the white linen on the headboard gives you that wonderful crispness,
which is very inviting in a bedroom. At night, the walls recede and all the
lights of the city come through the window, and it kind of sparkles."
—**BARBARA WESTBROOK, DESIGNER**

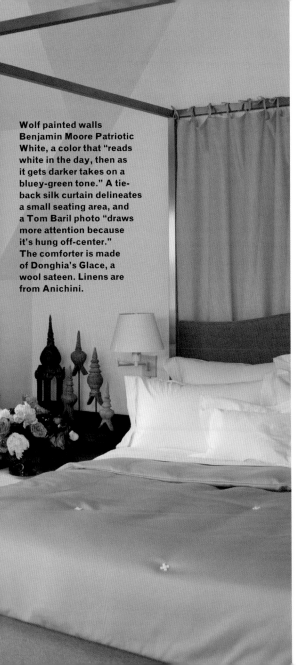

Wolf painted walls Benjamin Moore Patriotic White, a color that "reads white in the day, then as it gets darker takes on a bluey-green tone." A tieback silk curtain delineates a small seating area, and a Tom Baril photo "draws more attention because it's hung off-center." The comforter is made of Donghia's Glace, a wool sateen. Linens are from Anichini.

"I went to Papua New Guinea, and I saw this bird. It was a slatey blue. I kept it in my mind for five weeks. When I designed this bedroom, I thought, 'Boom! Let's use that color.'" —VICENTE WOLF, DESIGNER

....

"The bed curtains I like to use are sheer, transparent, seethrough. Here I used them to add a little soft texture against the edges of the steel frame. And they make the bed its own space—enveloped, like a tent."

....

"It's what I do with the bad things, the negatives, that makes the best statement. The positives work themselves out without me. The fireplace niche in the bedroom was a big negative—it's tiny, and the ceilings are high. How do you make it an intimate space? I used the little tieback curtain to create the feeling of a separate seating area."

BATHROOMS

ZEN | SCULPTURAL | MINIMAL

"We made the master bedroom and bath one space so the bathroom wouldn't read bathroom. It's more like a sitting room off the bedroom. The tub is a piece of furniture, floating there in front of the view." —VICENTE WOLF, DESIGNER

Clodagh Collection's Zen cast-concrete tub is on a concrete slab inside the glassed-in shower enclosure to make it "a sculptural focal point." Faucets and shower fixtures by Waterworks. Floors and walls are honed limestone.

"The turquoise blue is like the ocean just outside. And it's streaked with a little bit of white, which gives it a ripple. Everything in the room is sort of floating. The vanities and the tub are off the floor. It just looked so clean. We also wanted to bring in a natural element because the bathroom was getting sort of stark."
—MICHELE TROUT, DESIGNER

The vanity is topped with a slab of honed Thassos marble with a six-inch apron front. That gives it a little more heft, which suits the scale of the bathroom. A pretty, feminine mirror adds a few curves. A ceramic garden stool by the tub could hold a drink and a candle. "Everyone wants their bathroom to feel like a sanctuary," says Trout.

ACCESSORATOR

An audacious (yet perfectly composed) jumble of intricate pattern, vivid color and very personal collections

LEFT: "That little pink refrigerator is from an old company out of Italy. The funny part is that you order it through Sears. It's not really practical—it's more like a dorm refrigerator. But boy, is it cute."
—KRISTA EWART, DESIGNER

OPPOSITE: "I was driving by a store in L.A., saw this 1960s patio furniture, and screeched to a stop. It's modern without being stark, and it's petite—there's not a lot of room out here."
—KRISTA EWART

ENTRYWAYS

"I saw this sofa in a store and instantly fell in love with the modern-seeming, graphic Suzani pattern against that beautiful old wood. We don't really sit on it. My two dogs and two sons and their zillions of friends run by it on their way to another destination. I consider it art, really, so that's fine with me!"
—CHRISTINE GILLESPIE, DESIGNER

In this entry hall, graphic red and white Suzanis give an antique Swedish sofa from Indigo Seas a buoyant, modern look.

"I designed the stair runner to acknowledge the influence of arts & crafts—and its focus on nature—on Tudor style. I used leaves and vines and elongated them to make the design contemporary. It's one of my favorite things here."
—NANCY BOSZHARDT, DESIGNER

To the right of the stairs is a collection of African wood sculptures. Walls are Venetian plaster, waxed and hand done.

ENTRYWAYS

"Isn't that skirted table heaven? The thing that makes it so great is that they're not just dinky little grandma patches, they are big, big, big 18-inch patches. It drove my upholsterer insane. When you walk in and see that table, you know this house isn't going to be so traditional. It says that the owners are fun. They're patchwork people!" —T. KELLER DONOVAN, DESIGNER

The patchwork tablecloth is made of five different plaid and check fabrics.

"For me, beauty has to do with uniqueness. That's what I bring to the table. The compliment that means the most is when someone walks in and says, 'Wow, where on earth did you get that?'" —FRANK ROOP, DESIGNER

A collection of mirrored sconces adds sparkly charm to the entry alcove.

DESIGNER

Master class:
T. Keller Donovan

How do you deal with
a **BLANK WALL**?

"**Over a sofa it is
important to keep
your 'hang' from
looking static.
Try encircling a
sunburst mirror
with a set of prints.
One big gesture
is all it takes.**"

"**Over a fireplace, lean a
mirror off center, but give
it a sculptural companion
to keep things in harmony.
Top it with a small picture,
or two, to lift the eye, and
repeat over doorways or
tall chests.**"

"**On a big wall go for the
full-wall effect. If you have a
portfolio of eighteen monkey
prints (or a stack of photos of
your favorite pooch), frame
and hang them all uniformly—
even if some wind up below
eye level or behind the
furniture.**"

"In a hallway, run with a theme. Here, it starts with a chinoiserie mirror and a collection of ginger jars. Bamboo brackets—with lots of 'air' in between— give each jar individual attention, and make the collection more important."

"Over a nightstand create a grouping of dainty silhouettes to bulk up the profile of a skinny bedside lamp. Try a mirror in an old circular window over the headboard."

"Over a bed, buy four related prints and s-t-r-e-t-c-h them out along the wall: much more arresting than a skimpy pair, or the predictable block-of-four."

LIVING ROOMS

"I love stuff. I want to come home to more. I wanted a place for my books that would also function as an architectural anchor for the room, which it needed. But I really wanted the books, not the bookshelves, to be the big statement. And the gold ceiling is amazing when there are lots of candles here at night."
—JOE NYE, DESIGNER

The book-filled étagère is made of iron and wood. On top are three 1950s Los Angeles street scenes and cast-resin shell sculptures. Billy Haines side tables are from Dragonette; the vintage sofa, chairs, and coffee table are from Downtown.

"As William Morris said, 'Have nothing in your house that you do not know to be useful, or believe to be beautiful.' I have many beautiful objects, but I don't put them out all over the house all the time. It's easy to get carried away with accessories—I keep most of them in a closet, and rotate them. I also loan pieces to friends."
—MOISES ESQUENAZI, DESIGNER

A vintage **Suzani** and pillows designed by **Esquenazi** add a vibrant punch to the neutral sofa. A tray from **TableArt** holds flowers in a **Williams-Sonoma** silver tub; the orange and white dish is **Balcons du Guadalquivir** porcelain from **Hermès**.

LIVING ROOMS

"This is a classic American center-hall Colonial built around the turn of the century. Often when people buy old houses, they opt for a beige haze of graciousness. I looked at it and saw the potential for this traditional background to make a great foil for a graphic, groovy interior. It's a weekend house; bright, happy, informal, and unpretentious."
—JONATHAN ADLER, DESIGNER

"We went with a programmatic approach—the black and white foundation infused with single punches of color. In the living room, it's black and white with a splash of turquoise."

Adler designed most of the furnishings and accessories, including the living room's generous ottoman upholstered in Hinson's Montauk Texture in Aegean, the herringbone rug, and the black patent-leather Regent armchair. Knoll Barcelona chairs from Design Within Reach.

"We painted all the floors white, which is something I always love to do for instant happiness. Color is a great way to express playfulness."

COLOR CONSULTATION

ACCESSORATORS PICK THE HAPPIEST COLORS FOR LIVING ROOM
WALLS; DESIGNERS CHOOSE SOME OF THEIR FAVORITE HUES

JOHN YUNIS THINKS THE PERFECT SUNNY YELLOW IS FINE
PAINTS OF EUROPE SUNNYSIDE LANE 7014T
"It's hard to get yellow right—usually it's too green
or too red or too muddy. But this is nice and clear,
without being shrill. If it's too vivid, it's like living
in an omelette."

JAMIE DRAKE SAYS A CLOUDY DAY IS NO MATCH FOR
BENJAMIN MOORE SPARKLING SUN 2020-30
"In a long, narrow living room with windows at
only one end, I painted the walls with this super-
charged yellow. The light-bouncing high gloss
finish makes it feel as if sun is flooding the space,
even on the cloudiest of days."

SUSAN ZISES GREEN EVOKES A SMILE WITH DURON MT.
VERNON ESTATE OF COLOURS LEAMON SIRRUP DMV070
"This is the color of a pistachio nut—a clear, sharp
yellow-green with no sadness in it at all. I used it
in a showhouse for Kips Bay and there wasn't a
person who came in who did not smile."

EVERYTHING LOOKS DRAMATIC SILHOUETTED AGAINST RED
"Benjamin Moore Milano Red 1313 is a funny combination of pink and red and coral. Colors in that range are very stimulating—good for conversation, they keep people's minds going. It looks luscious in a satin finish. You can make most colors happy if you put enough sheen in the paint."
—**LIBBY CAMERON, DESIGNER**

LIVING ROOMS

SPLURGE ON THE DETAILS FOR BIG IMPACT

"My boyfriend calls it Disneyland. He says it's the happiest place on earth. The furniture is lighthearted, without a lot of hard edges. But I think it's the colors, patterns, and especially the dressmaker details on some of the classic pieces that bring it to a different place. I'm huge on the embellishments— the flanges, the trims, the welting." —MELISSA WARNER, DESIGNER

"There's a soft animal print, a floral, a geometric print, and an appliqué," Warner says. "All that variety makes it lively." Serena floor lamp by Oly. Ceramic stool from Forgotten Shanghai. Screen prints from Yolk. Walls are Soft Chamois by Benjamin Moore.

"I found this old textile book, and there was a lily-pad print from the 1920s. Something just clicked. The floor is the room's biggest surface area, so I thought, why not paint a pond? Besides, I was tired of all the geometric floors everyone's been doing."
—CHRISTINA MURPHY, DESIGNER

The floor's stylized lily pads were painted by Christopher Rollinson. The 1950s bentwood chairs are from Svenska Möbler.

LIVING ROOMS

ACCESSORIES MAKE A LIVING ROOM CHEERFUL, BRIGHT AND PLAYFUL

"I don't think you should ever restrain yourself! The more statement pieces, the better. I'm all for lots of accessories—they keep your eye moving around."
—KRISTA EWART, DESIGNER

"The living room bookshelves have this great original scallop detail. I designed the mirror over the fireplace to match."

"Anytime I see a great animal object with a good face, I have to have it—as long as it's got some age and soul. Anywhere I can sneak in an animal, I do."

In the living-dining area, armchairs covered in white linen with
pink piping from **Pindler & Pindler**
are a calming break from all the
pattern. The embroidered tablecloth,
from Mexico, is available at
Jacaranda Home.

"All the white
everywhere—
walls, ceiling,
woodwork—
allowed us to
have fun with
the fabrics."

"I use a polka-dot
fabric like a solid,
but it's a solid
with movement. It
excites your eye."

STYLE SEMINAR

with Eric Cohler

This New York City designer is known for his clever combinations of art and objects, high and low. His favorites are all about an Accessorator's idea of the good life.

1

2

6

1. **Lamp:** Any Christopher Spitzmiller lamp

2. **Alarm Clock:** Asprey

3. **Artist:** Mark Rothko

4. **Bed Pillow:** Frette goose down

5. **Car Color (exterior/ interior):** Sable gray/red

6. **Chair:** Klismos by Robsjohn-Gibbings

7. **Cleaning Supply:** Murphy Oil Soap

8. **Coffee or Tea:** Mariage Frères Yuzu Temple tea

9. **Color:** Mink brown

10. **Everyday Dishes:** Fishs Eddy Floorplan dinnerware

11. **Kitchen Gadget:** Cork Pops Legacy wine opener

12. **Lightbulb/Wattage:** PAR halogen 50W

13. **Mattress:** Hästens—firm, full size, special order brown-and-white check

14. **Pen:** Links of London fountain pen in engineturned sterling

15. **Picture Frame:** Pottery Barn lacquer in colors—orange, white, black. Mix the colors!

16. **Soap:** Molton Brown

17. **Stationery:** The Printery—chocolate and blue with yellow beehive

18. **Towel:** Greek key from Gump's in khaki

19. **Wallpaper:** White patent leather, Lacquered Walls #3852; Phillip Jeffries

20. **Workhorse Fabric:** Luke Twill by Lee Jofa in Cream

"I enjoy making still lifes of art and objects that speak to me—vignettes that mix old and contemporary. And I curate my clients' lives."
—ERIC COHLER

This 3-D still life atop a 1920s **William Kent**–style console includes a mid-century plaster maquette, a **Picasso** etching, and a sketch from a junk shop. Below the table is a 1958 **John Piper** painting. "I just like it down there, the fact that it's sort of peeking out at you," **Cohler** says. "It's like the wild lining inside a plain jacket. It also covers an ugly outlet."

LIVING ROOMS

FEMININE CURVES SOFTEN A ROOM'S HARD ANGLES

"We wanted it to be open, bright, fresh. The Egg comes from Design Within Reach." —ERIC COHLER, DESIGNER

Castel's Doero through Donghia on the Egg chair picks up the square shapes of the vibrant Donald Judd prints. Roman Thomas Palmer sofa, covered in Holly Hunt mohair. The coffee table is by John Boone. Lamps are from John Saladino.

A sofa covered in chocolate-brown linen velvet anchors the living room without stealing the limelight from the room's focal point: the layered mirrors. A Frances Elkins–inspired circle-back chair adds a touch of 1930s glamour, while a pair of Lucite and acrylic end tables designed by McGee have a more "modern edge."

"The bottom mirror is big so it really illuminates the room. But it's basic, with straight, modern lines. The top one, a Chippendale-style piece I found in an antiques store, adds dimension and a contrasting look." —MARY MCGEE, DESIGNER

INSPIRED OBSESSIONS

Tablescape

Dot goblet and glasses in acrylic from Macy's

Napkins from Rebecca Moses: Heart Soul Style through Macy's

Woven Two-Tiered Tray from Macy's

Murval through Ketzy's

Coupe Toile Plates through Macy's

Hampton Links earthenware by Jill Rosenwald through etsy.com

"My mantra: Mix patterns! Stick with one or two colors and you can't go wrong. I love polka dots and stripes together. Dots are so sophisticated—and so happy. We have to create happiness in our homes, and for me, the starting point is the table. I use herbs like flowers because I think a table should smell good—and they don't cost much." **—REBECCA MOSES, FASHION DESIGNER**

Ceramic plates, woven charger, napkin ring, flower dip-bowl, and metal lantern from Rebecca Moses: Heart Soul Style.

DINING ROOMS

"I must have repainted the dining room five times until I got it right. I was inspired by that John Fowler book. He'd have this 18th-century la-di-da furniture and then these wild colors. People must have gone crazy when they walked into his rooms." —GENE MEYER, DESIGNER

The dining room is painted Starburst Orange above the chair rail and Chartreuse below. The Brighton Pavilion–style wooden valance is painted Apple Green. All by Benjamin Moore. Wool-and-hemp Pleasure Palace rug designed by Doug and Gene Meyer for Niba Rug Collections.

"You can push the envelope in a dining room—you want it to be an experience, something exciting and sexy. The way the photo is printed on glass makes the colors glow. It's beautiful and romantic and earthy. I love a round dining table where you're all looking at each other. It's more intimate, and the conversation is better."
—THOM FILICIA, DESIGNER

Ralph Lauren Mango Gold paint was a last-minute touch to Filicia's Greek Peak chairs. Chairs and Bordino dining table, Thom Filicia Home for Vanguard Furniture. Karlin Hall lantern from DessinFournir. Curtains in Pomegranate in Grey from Lee Jofa. A Sacco mohair rug layered over sisal echoes the two-tone tabletop. Photograph by Roberto Dutesco.

DINING ROOMS

"This is a modern 1970s house with a lot of straight lines and enormous windows. We wanted to honor its era but make it feel warm and stylish, not dated. So in the daytime, the outside has to come in and be the star of the show. But when it's dark out, I wanted the room to still be interesting. So we tried to have a balance—not too busy, not too boring." —CHRISTINA MURPHY, DESIGNER

Murphy used a white lacquer table with rounded pedestal bases. For contrast, she lacquered Hickory Chair's fretwork chairs in chocolate brown. Cushions are Hable Construction's Viridian Palm linen.

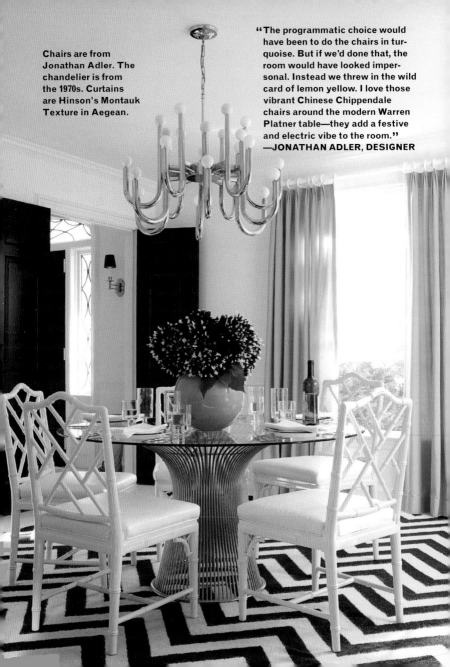

Chairs are from
Jonathan Adler. The
chandelier is from
the 1970s. Curtains
are Hinson's Montauk
Texture in Aegean.

"The programmatic choice would
have been to do the chairs in turquoise. But if we'd done that, the
room would have looked imper-
sonal. Instead we threw in the wild
card of lemon yellow. I love those
vibrant Chinese Chippendale
chairs around the modern Warren
Platner table—they add a festive
and electric vibe to the room."
—JONATHAN ADLER, DESIGNER

DINING ROOMS

"I wanted a warm and inviting setting that would accommodate antiques and fine objects without becoming precious. Banquettes give you the fun of pillows. And you don't have all those chairs grazing around like a herd of antelope."
—CELERIE KEMBLE, DESIGNER

"The room's definitely got a Mardi Gras flavor, a bit of surreal majesty! Paul Gruer's chandelier over the dining table centers the room. It's made of clay and crystal, but it reminds me of a tree in the forest right after the rain, with water dripping from it. I bought the curtains premade at Silk Trading Company. I love the sumptuous tangerine color. It looks like feasting to me!"
—KARYL PIERCE PAXTON, DESIGNER

A French neoclassical-style dining table, circa 1800, wears its original paint. Pulled up to it are Louis XVI–style chairs upholstered in a silk from ABC Carpet & Home.

DINING ROOMS

BRIGHT UPHOLSTERY SAYS "STAY A WHILE"

"Who wouldn't want to sit and relax around this big round dining room table? That bold, colorful chair fabric makes the serious mahogany table feel so casual and comfortable." —LYNN MORGAN, DESIGNER

Chinoiserie mural on the dining room walls by decorative artist Valerie Wall. Chairs covered in Bennison's floral Camelia on oyster linen surround a table from New Classics Collection through Holly Hunt. Niermann Weeks's Mansard Tole Lantern; AM Collections' Group23 Fretwork wool rug.

"The biggest mistake people make when they're trying to be colorful and exciting is to forget that you need to balance it with neutrals—otherwise it ends up looking like a color wheel. I like clear colors, like the paint you'd squeeze directly from the tube."
—TODD KLEIN, DESIGNER

A French farm table and whitewashed English Regency chairs sit on a Madeline Weinrib rug from ABC Carpet & Home. Blocks of bright color—on the chair seats and pillows—lend the room a playful air.

COLOR CONSULTATION

BRUCE BIERMAN TAKES A SHINE TO A CHAIR WITH PRATT
& LAMBERT AUTUMN CROCUS 1141

"This is a soft, muted lavender with a bit of blue
in it. I'd put it on a reproduction Louis XVI chair,
in high-gloss, because that's what makes it modern, and I'd find a fabric for it in exactly the same
shade—shiny, like a cotton chintz or vinyl."

KIM ALEXANDRIUK PUNCHES UP A BORING BED WITH
FARROW & BALL BABOUCHE 223

"In a guest room that seems a little staid, paint the
bed. This is a Ming yellow like you see in Chinese
silk robes, with a little lemon and mustard in it,
which gives it more dimension."

MOLLY LUETKEMEYER GIVES NEW LIFE TO A TOO-ORNATE
MIRROR WITH DUNN-EDWARDS AFTER THE STORM DE5769

"One of those inexpensive, gaudy mirrors with a
lot of carving can actually become quite beautiful
with paint. I like this deep, muted teal because it's
mysterious. You can't quite figure out if it's blue
or green. Colors like this with a little gray in them
take you to the next level of sophistication."

IT'S NOT A REAL CHINESE CHIPPENDALE CHAIR, BUT WHO CARES
WHEN IT'S PAINTED A DELICIOUS RED?

"I found this chair in Florida on the Dixie Highway and fell in love with the
high fretwork back. In brown it looked dreary, so I painted it pomegranate
red—Ralph Lauren Paint Relay Red IB11. It turned out so well I'm going to
reproduce it." —RUTHIE SOMMERS, DESIGNER

KITCHENS

TANGY | PIQUANT | TOOTHSOME

"You need harmony and balance, contrast, the right combination of elements, and scale. Symmetry and asymmetry. Light and dark. Like things with like things. And don't line objects up like they're on a march." —**DAN MARTY, DESIGNER**

The barn-wood cupboard doors, stove hood, and terra-cotta tile counter are original to the kitchen.

Lloyd Loom bar stools create
a breakfast spot at the marble-
topped kitchen island.

"We took out almost all the cabinets above the counters. I don't understand cupboards all closed up where all your things are put away. I make a point of using all of it because it seems silly to have all this stuff just to be on display. Why not use the fanciest bowl for your cereal? I mean, what's it for?" —PATRICK WADE, SENIOR V.P. OF CREATIVE FOR WEST ELM AND WILLIAMS-SONOMA HOME

INSPIRED OBSESSIONS

3-by-5-Foot Rugs; Small Bites

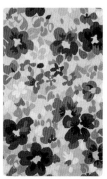

Giverny in Multi by Company C

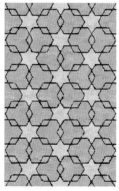

Petra in Chartreuse from Gary Cruz Studio

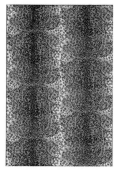

Majestic Leopard from Karastan

Newport Beach by Jean Larette through The Rug Finder

Malachite from Tony Duquette by Roubini Rugs

Persisk in Pattern 2 through IKEA

"You have to have harmony. I mean you see almost every room in one moment. You get a peekaboo of color from room to room that wraps it all up." **—KRISTA EWART, DESIGNER**

Kitchen rug is Lina from Plastica. A Dutch door opens to the children's room beyond. Stripes, polka dots, and big blue whales— a surprisingly companionable mix.

KITCHENS

LIVELY COLORS AND SHAPES MAKE
FOR A FUN FAMILY HANGOUT

Counter stools and trans.LUXE pendant light are in Alan Campbell's Potalla in Jungle Green. Shelves and Carrara marble countertops are amply stocked with Adler's pottery, including his giant stoneware horse bowl and lidded Apothecary of Emotion jars. The blue and white dishes are Villeroy & Boch.

"It's a room you want to be in because the outside is always close at hand—lots of green accents."
—JONATHAN ADLER, DESIGNER

"We upholstered the Norman Cherner stools and chairs in this lime-green print that's sort of crisply modern and floral-viney at the same time—perfect for the country. It's on the drum shade, too."

"We chose marble countertops and we used Ikea cabinets because . . . why not? They're well enough made. I think Ikea is a treasure. You can get a kitchen that looks this fabulous and not spend squillions."

"It's a sunny gathering spot with all the stuff you need for a modern family—most important of all, wireless computer reception. So it's computers going and cookies being baked and all the typical mayhem."

KITCHENS

"People like the idea of the kitchen being part of the entertaining space. I added the bookcase to make this kitchen feel more like an extension of the living room." —**THOM FILICIA, DESIGNER**

A geometrical arrangement of books on **Barrow** bookshelves from **Desiron**, layered with a painting by **Robert Moody**, creates a focal point in the kitchen area. Dark Jet Mist granite countertops play off light elm cabinets. **Karbon** faucet with five pivoting joints is paired with a **Bakersfield** sink, both by **Kohler**. Ceiling mount lights from **Visual Comfort**.

The contemporary Quimper dinnerware is still made in the original factory in France. The cabinets were custom-designed by Joanne Hudson. A collection of tea cozies is tucked on top. Old Italian apothecary jars line up on the marble countertop.

"I was looking through samples and I thought this color blue was warm and different, and would go well with my collections. The great feature of the house is my pottery, and I want to show it off. I couldn't live in one of those dull, ordinary kitchens with everything out of sight—that's no fun." —HILARY MUSSER, DESIGNER

"I have an Eero Saarinen side table next to a Frances Elkins dressing mirror. You need some contrast to rooms. When everything is of the same great pedigree, rooms look like museums. I didn't want my bedroom to look like Babe Paley's." —JOE NYE, DESIGNER

Nye says Claremont's George Spencer–Palm Stripe wallpaper was "a must-have."

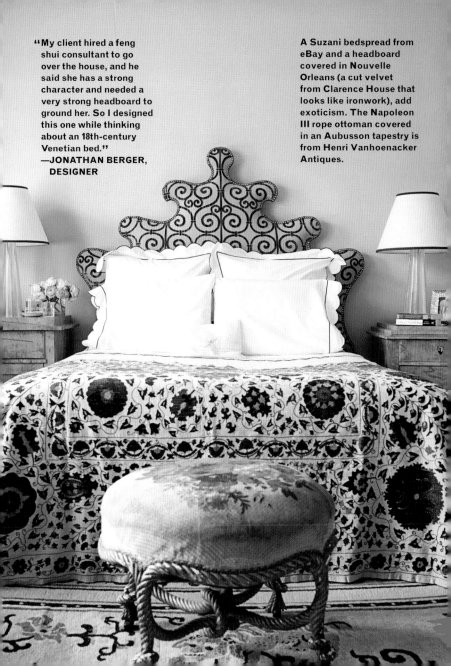

"My client hired a feng shui consultant to go over the house, and he said she has a strong character and needed a very strong headboard to ground her. So I designed this one while thinking about an 18th-century Venetian bed." —JONATHAN BERGER, DESIGNER

A Suzani bedspread from eBay and a headboard covered in Nouvelle Orleans (a cut velvet from Clarence House that looks like ironwork), add exoticism. The Napoleon III rope ottoman covered in an Aubusson tapestry is from Henri Vanhoenacker Antiques.

STYLE SEMINAR
with Barbara Hulanicki

This Miami decorator is also a fashion designer who understands the power of accessorizing. Take her advice to make stripes the perfect accessory for your boudoir.

COVER THE HEADBOARD IN WIDE VERTICAL STRIPES, DO A LARGE PILLOW IN THIN HORIZONTAL STRIPES AND THEN ADD THE SURPRISE OF BLACK AND WHITE STRIPED LAMPSHADES.

"I am always looking for invincible fabrics for headboards. Kalypso in Sand (top) from Kravet is indoor-outdoor, so you can keep it looking fresh without worry. Then it's good to throw in a stripe with another width for a large bed pillow like Tortola Stripe (bottom left) from Kravet. It gives the

look another dimension. For pillows and lampshades apply the stripes in different directions with Taglines in Ebony from Kravet (bottom right) for a great visual effect. It just goes to show—you don't have to be conventional when using stripes."

**MAKE A STRONG HORIZONTAL
STATEMENT WITH CURTAINS.**

"The big, bold stripes of Kalypso in Kahlua from
Kravet are dramatic and voluminous, which makes
the room feel cozy."

....

**UPHOLSTER AN ARMCHAIR, THE BACK IN VERTICAL
STRIPES, THE ARMS AND SEAT IN HORIZONTAL
STRIPES.**

"Of all the stripes, Melora Stripe in Sand/Terra-
cotta from GP&J Baker through Lee Jofa is a bit
brighter. I like a little punch of color, especially
on a smaller piece of furniture."

....

**VISUALLY PULL ALL THE STRIPES TOGETHER WITH
AN UPHOLSTERED BENCH AT THE END OF THE BED.**

"I love this fabric—Dilemma in Java from
Kravet! It contains all the colors used
throughout the room and visually pulls
everything together."

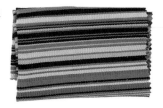

BEDROOMS

"The sheers at the windows diffuse the light, so the effect is all soft and dreamy like the old way they used to shoot movie stars—with Vaseline on the camera lens. It's the light every woman wants to be seen in." —CELERIE KEMBLE, DESIGNER

The bedroom is enveloped in silvery chinoiserie wallpaper and yards of silk and chenille, all from Brunschwig & Fils. Bench at window and small Lucite table at foot of bed, Niermann Weeks.

"I call this the Van Cleef bed because you see that quatrefoil motif on all those necklaces, but it's also an architectural motif that goes back centuries. Here, in sharp white against the gray, it looks very modern. And that rug is the animal print for people who don't really like animal prints, like me."
—THOM FILICIA, DESIGNER

The Asilah bed from Ironies, veneered in bone, is a cool white version of a traditional four-poster, shown with 800 thread count sheets by Hotel Collection in Mercury. Quilt from John Robshaw. Hobbs mirror by Julian Chichester. Seneca rug, Thom Filicia Home for Safavieh.

DESIGNER
Master class

How would you accessorize this tufted **WOODHOUSE HEADBOARD** from Jonathan Adler?

"When a bedroom calls for drama, this is the perfect headboard. Given that the shape is ornate and bold, I like the idea of upholstering it in rich velvet. For the tufting, I would use glittery vintage brooches in place of buttons. It'll up the design ante."

—**NATE BERKUS**

COTTON VELVET IN DUSK FROM HOLLY HUNT. VINTAGE BROOCH FROM CHICAGO VINTAGE UNDERGROUND.

"I'm having a fashion inspiration moment here with these cheerful Yves St. Laurent colors. A vertical pattern on this headboard could crush the height of a room, but the horizontal makes it nice and cozy. Keep the tufting and use the solid fabric for the border and welting."

—ROBERT COUTURIER

CAP FERRAT IN MULTI LILAC, PLUM, AND GOLD BY ALAN CAMPBELL THROUGH QUADRILLE, AND COUNTRY CLOTH IN PUMPKIN FROM QUADRILLE.

"I love the scale and simplicity of the headboard. Because it has such clean lines—I think of it as somewhat masculine—I'd choose a fabric that's more feminine. I would center the pattern. No tufting. It already has enough going on. Turquoise welting will give it a nice definition."

—MEG BRAFF

HENRIOT FLORAL IN TURQUOISE ON ECRU FROM QUADRILLE FABRICS WITH $\frac{1}{4}$" FRENCH PIPING IN SEA BLUE FROM SAMUEL & SONS.

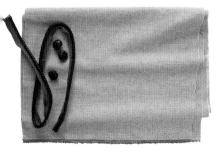

"This is a fanciful baroque form, and there's the danger of making it too sweet, too girly. So I'd go with a linen-y burlap texture and braided leather trim and buttons, which are a bit on the masculine side. They'll keep the man in your life from breaking out in hives when he sees the bed!"

—ERIC LYSDAHL

STRATUS SLUB IN PECAN FROM BEACON HILL, $\frac{3}{8}$" BRAIDED LEATHER CORD WITH TAPE IN MAHOGANY FROM SAMUEL & SONS. LEATHER KNOT BUTTONS IN BROWN FROM MJ TRIMMING.

BEDROOMS

"A silver leafed wooden deer head gives the room a sprinkling of out-there embellishment." —MOISES ESQUENAZI, DESIGNER

Big color works in a small space. Benjamin Moore Newburg Green on the walls plays off fabrics in hot tropical colors.

"The chocolate brown and the blue make me feel grounded. This blue reminds me of a day after it's rained, right before the sun comes out, when the ocean is so beautiful. Most clients would not have let me do this. I'm not sure I understood what I was doing, but I think it went somewhere wonderful, and I'm really thrilled with the way it came out." —ERIC COHLER, DESIGNER

Arrowroot grasscloth in Chocolate by Phillip Jeffries covers walls. Custom-painted lampshades echo the vibrant Suzani throw on the bed: "My ode to Matisse," says Cohler. The suede-covered headboard is Cohler's own design. The ceiling is Phillip Jeffries Sapporo Linen wallpaper in Blue.

BATHROOMS

"The predominant feeling of white makes it feel really clean. The green adds life. What I love about the wallpaper is that it looks handmade. You can see painted brushstrokes on the ferns. It's fun to look at it for a long time, and what better place than a bathtub, where you can soak and stare?"
—CHRISTINA MURPHY, DESIGNER

A freestanding Empire tub by Waterworks is positioned under a skylight. Fern wallpaper by Spring Street Designs creates an instant tropical rain forest.

Hinson's
Fireworks
wallpaper by
Albert Hadley
highlights a
mirror Ewart
designed. Light
fixture from Old
School Lighting.
Pottery Barn
towels.

"The bathroom is hilarious: It's so tiny, there's only the little sink and a shower. But this polka-dotty print with the pink herringbone shower curtain just makes me happy." —KRISTA EWART, DESIGNER

INDEX

PHOTO CREDITS

HEARST BOOKS
New York

An Imprint of Sterling Publishing
387 Park Avenue South
New York, NY 10016

Copyright © 2011
by Hearst Communications, Inc.

Book design by Nancy Leonard

Library of Congress Cataloging-in-Publication Data
Cregan, Lisa.
  House beautiful style 101 : a handbook to the five essential looks for the home you'll love / Lisa Cregan.
      p. cm.
   Includes index.
   ISBN 978-1-58816-883-2
   1. Interior decoration. I. House beautiful. II. Title. III. Title: House beautiful style one hundred one. IV. Title: House beautiful style one hundred and one. V. Title: Handbook to the five essential looks for the home you'll love.
   NK2115.C94 2010
   747–dc22

                              2010046173

10 9 8 7 6 5 4 3 2

House Beautiful is a registered trademark of Hearst Communications, Inc.

www.housebeautiful.com

For information about custom editions, special sales, premium and corporate purchases, please contact Sterling Special Sales Department at 800-805-5489 or specialsales@sterlingpublishing.com.

Distributed in Canada by Sterling Publishing
c/o Canadian Manda Group,
165 Dufferin Street
Toronto, Ontario, Canada M6K 3H6

Distributed in Australia by Capricorn Link (Australia) Pty. Ltd.
P.O. Box 704, Windsor, NSW 2756 Australia

Manufactured in China

Sterling ISBN 978-1-58816-883-2